Comprehensive Guide to Private Money Markets

How to prepare & borrow from the private money markets

Anthony A. O' Brien

DEDICATION

To my Wife, Kelly. She stands by me through thick and thin, my best friend, my spouse and my best cheerleader. I would never have gotten this project done without her love and support.

CONTENTS

ACKNOWLEDGMENTS

This book is the result of a great many years of experience in Private Money Finance. When I decided to take the time to put this book together my goal was to share the lessons I have learned through my lengthy career in this unique and extremely rewarding market place with you, my readers and potential private money borrowers.

I understand the miserable experience of taking my business model to the local bank only too well. On numerous occasions, I have received the obligatory smile, thanking me for my loyal patronage and deposits but told, "no, I'm sorry, we don't lend on these types of projects."

I hope that you will take what I have collated here – namely, the wisdom of many victories and some defeats in the private lending business – and use the teachings to help create the life that you have always dreamed of for yourself, your family and loved ones.

In my mind, there is no greater opportunity for the creation of wealth than acquiring real estate, rehabbing the property, and either selling or holding as a long-term rental. As stock markets, commodities, hard assets and even real estate prices rise and all – sometimes violently – people will always need a safe, affordable home to live in. The real estate rental market, as well as the owner-occupied market, will be around as long as you're alive, and best of all, no market is closed to your effort, and no major corporation or empire can move you aside. There is no manipulation of market pricing in this industry; just plain old American ingenuity and hard work. The banking industry may have proven itself to be unreliable when it comes to lending money for your projects, but private money markets are robust and growing into a reliable source for capital. If you follow the advice I share in this book, you will be able to negotiate the private money market with precision and speed.

Enjoy the journey you're about to take!

Anthony A. O'Brien

1 INTRODUCTION

I never considered myself a professional until I quit my well-paid job. I was working as a Senior Vice President at Bache Halsey Stuart Shields – which would later become Prudential Bache Securities – and moved to California to start a trading firm and hedge fund. Now that I was alone I felt like a true professional; an entrepreneur, forced to live off my intuition and skills to put food on my table and grow my wealth.

Since then, I have spent a considerable amount of time in the securities, energy and real estate industries. It's the latter where I find the best place to exercise my entrepreneurial spirit without limitations or roadblocks, as the real estate market provides so many avenues in which one can seek their fortune. You can look no further than the block you live on, or branch out and investigate the opportunities in any one of our great fifty states. You can focus on rural areas, suburbia, or the heart of a city. Perhaps most importantly, price is controlled by supply and demand; real estate is the last market not to be manipulated by big government, or an algorithm that can beat your price by seconds to an electronic trading screen.

Everybody has the same advantage except one, and unfortunately that's a doozy; access to money. Anybody can rehab a property after doing their homework to find the asset, but not everybody can borrow money successfully. Many factors come into play when you start asking for financial assistance, and this book is not about having money. It's about *borrowing* money in the spirit of investment opportunity.

During the early years of my career, which were spent trading the equity markets, I learned the path that giant trading firms such as Goldman Sachs, Bear Stearns and Merrill Lynch controlled the path I travelled. Although they would allow the small trader to succeed, we were merely a backdrop – a useful resource to lay off their bad deals. We could exist and make money, but not *real* money. Not the kind of money the big firms pulled down each and every year. Impediments such as market manipulation, control of capital as to how much we could leverage and government intervention slowly destroyed the equity market – to the point that we no longer see this place as a viable arena for creativity or independence.

On the other hand, real estate is the last frontier for making the kind of money we have all dreamed about, short of creating the next Amazon, Apple or Uber. There are no walls blocking your path to success. From the great real estate barons of the past to today's successful titans, all made their fortune in the real estate markets, starting small and growing their empires one step at a time.

How did they do it? Well, they had something we lacked. Not talent, hunger or ambition – the one thing the big funds and top investors have that we lack is the access to capital. The banks fawn over these elitists, throwing capital at them without shame, *begging* these titans to take their funds.

The adage, "you can't borrow money until you don't need it," is very true when it comes to the banking industry. Thankfully a new strategy is booming right before your very desk; private money markets are primed and ready to lend. This market doesn't require you to put on a suit and tie, or an expensive dress. It doesn't even require you to get into your car and drive a great distance to be received. You can borrow 100% of the time sitting at your desk, wearing whatever you desire, and arranging capital to buy and rehab your next real estate project.

The mistake you are making pertains to the amount of time you spend chasing capital, driving from bank to bank with hat in hand, begging for someone to buy into your business model. The fact is, you are limited by the amount of time you have to seek your financing *and* continue working your day job. You simply can't continue to do all the work to acquire money, while each property you have your eye on disappears to another investor who is already funded. After all, if you spotted potential, it's safe to assume that one of your rivals did the same.

I know that, deep down, you desire to quit your nine-to-job job and jump into the real estate market with both feet. You imagine driving from one property to the next, watching how your contractors are performing, converting that $85,000 property into a lovely owner-occupied home that you plan on selling for $125,000 in the coming months. There is only one thing standing in your way of success; capital, or a lack thereof.

"You see," I figured out, "as long as I have capital I can buy, rehab and sell as many properties as I can handle." Anybody can create a successful borrowing program, including *you*. What you need is the knowledge of how to borrow money in the private lending markets, what to say, what you will need to show the lenders, and how much you can expect to borrow.

Banks will become what they should be – places to hold your money, federally insured, as you go to the private money markets for capital.

Reading this book is your first step toward financial freedom and success. Once completed, you will have every confidence of what you need and how to present your project for funding. If you have financial challenges or legal issues, no problem; you will understand why you can't borrow funds, but you will understand what it takes for you to add the necessary partner or family member that will allow you to step to the borrowing window. The banks may have closed their doors in the face of real estate investors, but private money markets are standing with their arms wide open. This book is about success – *your* success – and not a book about why you can't succeed.

Let's take this journey together.

Tony O'Brien

2 WHAT IS PRIVATE MONEY?

This book is being written so you, the investor, can come to a complete understanding of the private money markets. After you have finished reading you will understand exactly what you need to do, how to do it, and what to expect from your lender. You need to embrace the private money markets, as banks have abandoned America – without private money, you and every other investor would be outside the tent looking in. Enjoy this education, as nobody else in our lending industry will be as forthright or complete in detail.

"Hard Money," sounds so ominous. It conjures images of the type of guy you would see in a movie, who breaks your legs if you refuse to repay the loan in 30 days, mumbling, "Forget about it." I promise that such slang terms used by wise guys will not show up here again; this book is going to unlock all the information you need to move around the private money markets with success, on both your functioning, resolutely unbroken legs.

I prefer the terms "private money, non-conventional money, Outside Dodd Frank or even reliable money." After all, most of the time your local commercial bank is "hard money," am I right? You will learn to hate the banks as much as the IRS if you try to go through one of their lending programs. Most times you will walk away following a bad experience in which you threatened to pull every dime you have in their institution, returning home angrier then most bad golfers. All for what?

The reality is, private money markets are willing to lend you the finance you need quickly, at times of an aggressive interest rate. All you'll need to do is meet the necessary criteria to make a positive impact on your real estate lender. Along the way, you will most likely create a personal relationship with your new best friend that will last for years, or until you move on to other forms of investing.

3 PRIVATE VS. CONVENTIONAL LENDING

First, let's define both terms so there can be no confusion. A *conventional* lender is any Federally-funded bank, savings and loan, credit union or other financial institution that does more than lend. If an establishment provides you with a checking account or savings account and they also have a mortgage department, you're dealing with a conventional lender. Anybody who is backed by FDIC provides conventional lending, and anybody who writes "owner occupied' mortgages are in fact a conventional lender. The key point to understand, when dealing with conventional lenders, is that your personal income and W2 statements are all they care about. If you don't have good, solid W2 income, the chances of getting a successful loan from a conventional lender is as likely as Katy Perry or Henry Cavill calling you for a date.

Private lenders, meanwhile, are entrepreneurial like you. They create markets in order to borrow capital and lend to you. Since 2008, when the real estate market blew up, every bank in America has closed their doors to real estate risk. In their absence, the private money markets have thrived.

Private Lenders don't obtain their funding from the Federal Reserve or bank depositors, but from private sources such as hedge funds, crowd funding, insurance companies, and private investors willing to tender their money for a fixed rate. The private moneylender then marks that money up and loans it to real estate investors; the embodiment of what I call the "American Spirit of Pure Capitalism."

For the most part, no government oversite, whatever the market, will sign off on a quick and gentle promise. "I'll give you this much, you give me this much back," all wrapped up within a couple weeks and a few conversations. Beautiful, right? But also, littered with its own business style, vocabulary, paperwork and requirements. When you finish reading this E-Book you will be a "private money expert," complete with a solid game plan, focus, and understanding how to make the private money system work for you successfully every time you find a new property. With all that in mind, let's get started.

Private money will lend on every aspect of real estate. We both know that your local bank will *not* provide an acquisition/rehab loan, bridge loan or a transactional funded deal. You *can* get a conventional loan – if you have W2 income, a strong 700+ credit score, and a relationship with your banker that will afford you an opportunity to ask for a 30-year mortgage. The fact is, investment property owners are left out in the cold when it comes to conventional lending programs.

There are Four Main Lending Programs in the Private Money Sector.

1. **Acquisition/Rehab**: Used for purchasing real estate assets to be rehabbed and either sold as an owner-occupied property or rented to a tenant. Funding is usually a one-year interest-only loan, with rates starting at 8-15%, depending on your credit score and experience.

2. **Bridge:** Used to acquire a property that requires little or no rehab effort. Property would be either sold or offered as a rental. Like Acquisition/rehab funding, the loan is one-year interest-only loan, with the rates and requirements similar to acquisition/rehab funding.

3. **Transaction Funding:** This is a specialty loan used mainly by wholesalers and flippers. Funding for a period less than 24 hours, usually a simultaneous close that is also known as back-to-back closing. A bank will never offer this loan, but the private money markets will. Your cost of funds is predicated on the selling price of the property, usually 1-1.5%

4. **Term Loan Mortgage:** this is a 30-year amortized mortgage which is written to take out short funding or refinancing for cashing out, or a purchase that is tenant ready. Private money will not write a mortgage to an individual buying a property for their own use, owner occupied; this type of mortgage is strictly for investment properties.

The private money market will provide you all the necessary capital to succeed. You and I are going to cover every lending segment in detail, as well as what you can expect when you approach the private money market and the level of success you can rely on.

Private money lending focuses on the asset, also known as "asset based" lending. In other words, the asset valuation of the property carries more weight than your credit score.

4 ACQUISITION & REHAB FUNDING

Many call this a "fix and flip" loan, but personally I hate that term as much as I hate, "hard money" The label itself makes the effort you're involved in sound so *sleazy* – like, "hey, anyone can do this!" We both know that is not the case. You have taken great pains to find the right property, worked up the rehab budget, and done your due diligence on the "ARV" (After Repair Value). Just an aside – learn this term, as it's critical to your success. You'll learn more about why, and what these terms mean to you, shortly. Finally, you know how long it's going to take you to complete the project; you can tell from the effort and time you spent. As I outlined there is nothing about "fix and flip" in our conversation. I prefer to call this segment, "acquisition/rehab" funding for the obvious reasons. The term speaks to a professional effort, and identifies the person involved in this process as a professional.

Let's begin with the necessary image you will need to project. 100% of the time, you will be communicating your needs by telephone and a computer. My head office is located in beautiful Lake Norman North Carolina, but we lend in 40 States. I can honestly say, of the thousands of loans I have made, I have only met one client in person. You can wear blue jeans and dirty T-shirts to your job every day, if that's your preference-there's no need to take your suit to the dry cleaners.

However, if you're trying to borrow 85% of your investment and 100% of your rehab costs, I suggest you adopt a professional demeanor on the telephone and computer from the outset. Always keep in mind you're asking a stranger to lend you thousands of dollars and to trust your judgment and professionalism. Many borrowers come forward, but few come away with the funding they need.

I will start with the premise you have found the right property to acquire, and you have created a working budget – or at least written down the necessary rehab work to complete the task. Now let's talk about the next, most critical step: the funding process for an acquisition/rehab loan.

5 PRESENTATION

You will need a copy of your purchase contract, rehab budget, investment experience and a game plan when you connect with a lender. You will be asked to complete an application, and each lender is different depending on who you're working with. Plan on filling out a *lot* of paperwork until you find the right lender who you click with. When a new investor connects with my company, Real Estate Lender USA, the process is the same every time.

1. Application.
2. Copy of the purchase contract.
3. Rehab budget.
4. Investment background, outlining your projects over the previous two-years.

My biggest complaint when dealing with investors is laziness and lack of information. If you provide an application our on-boarding team are unable to read, we're already seeing you as an unprofessional – or worse, somebody with something to hide. You need to keep reminding yourself that you are asking to borrow thousands of dollars. I always recommend to my clients that they pretend they're applying for their dream job. Would you provide a partial, poorly written resume? Could you see yourself with a partially completed employment application put together in a haphazard way, or would you be putting your best penmanship to use? More is better, when it comes to information about yourself.

Also, use the right software. We all have Microsoft Word – that will fill in your application with a font that can be read by the lender and their team. If the line asks for your birthdate, put the information in. Yes, we need your social security number, because we will eventually run your credit. Every question we ask is critical.

These questions are there to allow a swift and clear understanding who we are working with. What is your experience, do you have the capital behind you, and can you perform? As mentioned earlier, you and I will most likely never meet face-to-face. We have you on the phone for short period of time, and your paperwork is the initial test to discover who you are, and whether I wish to lend to you.

There are no shortcuts to this process – put your paperwork together *before* you approach a lender. If you want that loan in 14 days, it will take your undivided attention to detail in order to succeed. Finally, and this is very important – we *all* hate paperwork. If you're talking to multiple lenders, you will need to complete multiple applications. This may seem like an endless task of penmanship, but I assure you it is critical that you approach this step as though you are mining for gold. Those first couple days of digging into a mountain is duller than dishwater, but then you hit the vein and Eureka! Eventually the paperwork ends, and if accepted and a term sheet is issued, the journey begins. Let's take a walk through a typical transaction and how you will respond to the lenders requests.

6 THE PROCESS

OK, you have gotten your application in, the lender likes what he sees, and now you've been asked for two critical items; a purchase contract for the property you're buying, and your rehab budget. These two items will make or break your loan process as from this information, the lender will be issuing you a term sheet outlining what they are willing to lend you based on your preliminary information, purchase contract and rehab budget.

If you have no property at this point and your intention is to get through the underwriting process so you can obtain a "commitment letter," be sure to inform your lender of this decision. Some lenders will not start the process until you have a property to buy, <u>Real Estate Lender USA</u> on the other hand believes this decision is sound and should be rewarded with a commitment letter.

7 THE PURCHASE CONTRACT

This will tell us where you're buying, how much the asset will cost, and whether you are financially capable of handling the investment. Ensure that both buyer, and seller have signed the contract, and that it's legally binding so we can rely on the information. When you negotiate the purchase contract with a seller, be sure you're allowing yourself enough time to close the loan. Typically,

you will need at least three weeks for an acquisition/rehab loan, though we *can* get to the closing table in 14 days – provided you have the available information ready to send, and an appraiser is available. You will be shocked; in some markets, we must wait a fortnight for an appraiser to go out and do their job, mainly due to a staff shortage or heavy demand. After the first deal, you can expect to close with the same lender within 10 days or less.

Too often I receive a purchase contact with a closing date two or three weeks in the future. Why would you put that kind of pressure on yourself? Use the clause, "subject to arranged financing," or the equally helpful, "45 days or sooner." This will allow you to go through the underwriting process successfully and close on time. You need to allow yourself a month the first time, which is really 20 working days, regardless of what anyone tells you; a month includes 7 days to complete an appraisal, a necessary task each time.

Finally, when you're signing a purchase contract, be sure you provide yourself with "outs" during the negotiation. Don't get hooked with a non-refundable escrow. If you must do non-refundable, ensure it is a very small deposit. Use the inspection process, which we are going to cover during the rehab segment, as a pullout option; you can also use the appraisal as a viable excuse to cancel. If your inspection brings to light a very bad structural problem, you need to walk. If your appraisal fails to support your purchase price or after repair value, the money you're asking for will not come through. These are both good reasons to cancel and have your escrow money returned. Keep in mind that you can also schedule an inspection before you go to contract.

8 REHAB BUDGETS

These can be tricky, and can make or break any deal. Once again, I suffer from investors who provide me *just* enough information without any evidence of reality. They submit budgets as though we can look at it and say, "sure I get the message. Let me write the check."

Your rehab budget is part of the total loan being made to you. If you tell me that you need $15,000 to rehab your asset and the appraiser comes back and says, 'no way" – guess what, you're out. Another example we run into is a client providing a rehab budget for $9,000 which we approve and loan the funds. During the rehab period the client realizes the work is going to cost $14,000. Well, bad news – that one is on you, brother. Once the loan is made and the first lien on the property is filed, we can't go back and change the loan. And of course, we see this all the time; a client requests $23,000 for rehab, we lend it, and the actual effort takes $15,000 Bummer, you're paying interest on funds that you have no use for. That surely does hurt the old wallet.

I will say this again – *your rehab budget will make or break your project.* Don't be conservative, or aggressive. Be *accurate* Rely on professional contractors, whom you have interviewed and reviewed their credentials, before you make an offer on a property. Nothing is worse than having an offer accepted when you still don't have a clue what the rehab costs will set you back. Lenders make *one* loan, covering rehab and acquisition, and getting your rehab budget correct is a key component to a successful loan.

When we send in an appraiser, he is going to have your completed rehab budget in hand. That anticipated work would allow the appraiser to provide the ARV (After Repair Value), which is a critical number when seeking this type of loan. Many deals have failed because the overstated rehab budget pushed the *real* rehab expense to the point that the project was a bust after completion. On the other side of a bad deal, you're buying a house for $78,000 and the rehab budget is $60,000, Outside of California that deal will not close. The fact is, that deal is not a rehab – it's a teardown, and lenders *hate* teardowns. A good ratio to remember is that we are not going to lend more on a deal that has a rehab budget of 50% or higher of the purchase price.

Your chosen property has two values as it sits; current value and After Repair Value. Though an acquisition loan is lending the money you seek based on the current value of the property and the rehab budget you have submitted, we rely on the ARV to confirm the loan size. A qualified loan will be equal to or less than 70-75% of the ARV.

Example: You're buying a property for $120,000, with a rehab budget of $22,000. This sounds like a nice deal so far. We go through the paperwork, all the background checks, document production and we order the appraisal. You have provided a nice tight rehab budget showing the necessary work you want done and found the right contractor to work with, things are looking good. Then the appraisal comes back with an ARV of $145,000. Ouch, now what?

Originally, the lender had agreed to lend you 80% of acquisition price and 100% of your rehab budget – $118,000. Now, with the ARV at $145,000, you can only borrow 70% - which drops the loan to $101,500, and you will be expected to make up the difference. The ARV is also a good indication of your expected selling price once the work is completed if you plan on flipping the property. Now is the time to ask yourself if you want to move forward with additional money from your own pocket to close the loan?

The example above is a bad deal, and you need to cancel. Too many times my clients get "married" to a project; they want to believe their numbers are correct, and the appraiser has screwed up. My suggestion is that you trust and believe someone other than yourself when it comes to areas of expertise you have no background in. The appraiser is most often right on their comps, which is the primary block of information lenders are going to scan to insure the appraisal has the right integrity to trust. If you had run your own comps, or had your real estate broker run comps on the property before you entered into a contract, you will know what those numbers are going to reflect. If the appraiser comes back with lower comps than you did, you have the right – and we will support you – to refute the appraisal, offering your comps as evidence the appraiser got it wrong. I never had an appraiser not agree to reconsider his comps against. those that you and your broker or consultant used, and they will alter their view in your favor.

The most obvious reasons for discord between your comps and the appraiser are square footage, bedrooms, bathrooms, location and lot size. I see too many clients bring comps to the table for properties that are listed rather than sold, which is a big no-no. Don't allow your broker to show you comps of properties *being* sold in your area vs. sold in your area. Also, if you're intending on selling that property after you have rehabbed it, you want to know how long properties like yours have been on the market for sale. If you're seeing 90-120 days before selling, you better plan on paying interest on your money during that waiting time. If you're paying the lender $800 a month and your property is going to sit for three months, that will cost you $2,400 of profit.

You need to address the ARV *before* you place your offer on the property, and again after you do a work up on your rehab budget. There is little or no flex in the ARV, and you only have two choices – make up the difference, or walk away. Imagine if you had made an offer on a property, placed non-refundable earnest money on the table, and these events play out? This is a very expensive lesson; one that's better to learn here and now and thus avoid the disaster facing you later.

If you plan on keeping the property as a rental, you will have one added step – figuring out the rental income you can expect to receive in the market where your property resides. This step is often forgotten step by new investors, and there is nothing worse than buying and rehabbing a property, then finding that your rental assumptions were way off the mark. I had to scuttle an entire package of duplexes I was building because the rent we had factored into the project of $1,250 per month, per side, came in at $900 per month, per side. *Ouch.* What a mess would I have been in had I written the check for the $165,000 I needed to build?

9 THE TERM SHEET

So, your purchase contract is in the lenders hands, along with your buttoned-up rehab budget. What happens next, if the lender likes what he sees, is the issue of a term sheet (some call this an LOI, or Letter of Intent)

This is where the rubber meets the road, my friend. Now you will see – in writing – if the rate the lender quoted you and the terms of the loan have stayed the same or moved in another direction. Your fees are disclosed, and the rate and loan size will all be spelled out in this document. You will be asked to sign, showing that you have reviewed the information the lender has provided you and that you agree on all terms and conditions. This is the last time you will get to negotiate your terms with the lender. This is also the time you will ask questions pertaining to every last detail of the loan and why certain charges are being applied.

You might be asked to pay an application fee – this is standard. Some lenders charge it on the back end, and some ask for it prior to the underwriting process. There is a *lot* of effort to insure your paperwork meets the standard the lender requires to draw on his capital to lend to you, and in my experience, three in ten loans will fail due to circumstances not noticed by lender or client. The application fee allows the lender to do the work necessary to get your file to the final approval stage.

Every document you submit will be reviewed, confirmed and either accepted or rejected with further information needed. There will also be times that you are asked to explain an issue that appears on your credit report, such as a prior bankruptcy, an issue on another property you own, or a credit issue. What we will ask from you is a letter of explanation, or LOE. As you are moved down the underwriting channel, you will be provided a short list of corrections or required documents to be submitted, which is known as the conditions stage. Many clients grow frustrated during this process, but don't allow it to bug you. I always tell my clients that if they were not being asked for this information, there would be no interest in providing the loan.

10 NECESSARY DOCUMENTATION

Aside from the initial application, purchase contract and rehab budget, other documents you will be asked to furnish are two months of bank statements, a list of other properties you own or have completed which helps with experience, clean LLC or corporation, along with the operating agreement or corporate articles of incorporation, you EIN number, identification such as a driver license or passport. Stay away from no document loans – your rates are going to be very high, and the effort of repaying them will be borderline suicidal. Gather the necessary documents now, put them in a file, and be ready to send this information on your next deal. Quick, easy and professional.

Credit scores are the single most important tools you can bring to the table. Lenders don't care if you have $500,000 in the bank and a credit score of 580, as this means you will be paying cash for your property. If you're looking to operate purely on finance however, most lenders will not drop below a score of 620, regardless of how many bottles of wine you ship them. If you have a business partner with a credit score below standard but you have a stellar number of 720, guess what – lenders go by the lower score. Remember the old saying, "the weakest link in a chain." If this event with a partner does occur, and this is important, drop him or her from the LLC or corporation and use only the strongest credit score. Your loan will move quickly through the process to a successful conclusion. You and your partner can sort out the business side of the relationship in a separate agreement.

One final note on credit scores. Lenders use the mid score, not the highest number shown. There are three reporting credit agencies, each put out a score. Let's say your numbers are 680 – 730 – 760. We would use 730 as your "mid score." It is great to subscribe to a free credit reporting service, as this will help you monitor your numbers. Understand this though – our numbers are not based on retail reporting, which is what free credit score programs offer. We rely on a deeper, more meaningful report that includes mortgage payments. Don't be surprised as you proudly announce to me that your credit score is 750 and it comes back as 705. At Real Estate Lender USA, we also offer a free service to our clients to assist in boosting your credit score. We have a service that will run your credit and recommend what needs to be done in order to get a bump in your score – very helpful for clients who are teetering on the edge of approval.

We also have a program at Real Estate Lender USA that will pre-approve our clients before they find a property, which is very popular with smart people. We do the full underwriting, issuing a commitment letter for an agreed amount of funds they will need, and the investor knows immediately what their purchase threshold is. This early effort knocks two weeks off the underwriting process and assures success. For seasoned investors, we offer you a line of credit that allows a swift closing once an appraisal comes back.

11 EXPERIENCE

Experience is a key factor when you're looking to borrow money. For several years, I was an aspiring actor, and every thespian wants to be a member of SAG, the Screen Actors Guild. In order to be a member, you had to either have a speaking role in a union sponsored film or an extended time on camera in a cameo role – but you can't get a speaking role in a film or that cameo role *unless* you're a member of SAG. See the dilemma? Borrowing funds from the private lending market is much the same way. We don't want to lend to beginners, but everyone has to start somewhere, so how do you borrow needed funds? This is a tough road that I cross several times a month with new clients. Fortunately, this means I have plenty of advice on how to beat the newbie tag and achieve success.

I *will* lend to a new investor under certain conditions, and a good project helps most of all. Bringing a solid, professionally presented project, showing that you have your paperwork squared away, will eliminate some of the sting of being new to the process. Whatever you do, *don't* connect with a lender as a new investor, looking to buy a quad that needs a full rehab. Put bluntly, that isn't going to happen. There are proven ways around this issue, however.

Finding a qualified investor/mentor that you can team up with on your first few deals is one successful way to get past the newbie tag. Don't be afraid of this approach; I personally financed a large 7-unit apartment building with a new investor who teamed up with a well-qualified partner and a huge investor on his own. The loan went through, the new investor learned a lot about our industry and the project was a huge success.

Another major key to success is ensuring there is more than enough funding for the whole project. As a new investor, you need to show strength, and cash in the bank does that for you. I will take on a new investor if he can show me he has plenty of funds beyond what is needed to purchase and rehab the property. How much do you need? 20-30% more than the project will cost is a good number to start with. Cash is king, and it's your ace in the hole as a new investor. If you come to me with a good asset but insufficient money to make the deal work, it is doomed to failure. I don't lend money on the deal; I lend money to the *capable investor.*

Also, let me reiterate the importance of your credit score. As a new investor, ensure you're reflecting a strong credit score, as this is another factor in making the loan. Don't be shy about being a first-time investor, as we all started out that way, but do get it out in the open, asking point blank and early in the process, "will you work with first time investors?" Many lenders say, "no," but others, like us, will say, "yes, under certain conditions." Understand these conditions, and try to meet the necessary qualifications early into the process. There is nothing more frustrating than going through the underwriting process and hearing you're not qualified because you haven't done 3 deals in the past 12 months. If you hear the lender will work with you, ask what your rate is going to be and the points up front. I have seen lenders suggest a rate of 10%, only for the term sheet to arrive and quote 13%.

You hear all these great stories from webinar coaches trying to entice you by promising that you will never need to use your own money. Exactly whose money are you going to use? Don't even think you're borrowing 100% of the purchase price; that doesn't happen, even on Warren Buffet's best day. Lenders want you to have a stake in the effort. The best loan I will make is 90% of the acquisition price, to a well-qualified heavy hitter. You will be doing well if you can borrow 70% of the acquisition price and a large portion of the rehab budget early in your investment career. Like any other great career, the better you perform, the more funding you can borrow and the lower your interest rate will be. Don't get angry because what you expected didn't occur; we all started from point A. You will too, and as time and deals go by, the costs you incur by doing business will go down.

The most important quality you can offer any lender is your credibility. My biggest concern, and the toughest calls we take at the office, come from new investors asking us to lend on a major project such as a 10 or 20-unit apartment building, or 20 run down houses, or an even bigger asset like a major real estate development. Forget about the fact that your closest experience in these projects may be the fact you once lived in or near something like your request.

My first question is always, "how many apartment buildings do you currently own?" Here is a major hint; if you have been buying single-family homes your entire investment career or this is your first effort and suddenly you want to take on what we would consider a major project, you will not find the money you need. That's like running up a good score at the batting cage and expecting the Yankees to hand you a start at the double-header that weekend. You will need to move up through SFR properties a few times, showing success, then go find a duplex or a triplex, then maybe a quad. Onward and upward, that is a traditional investment migration. Your previous experience is a key factor to us, or indeed anybody else loaning you the required funds. More or bigger is not better; risk needs to be mitigated, and putting the right investor into the right project will help lenders do that. Lenders want to loan on good deals, not dreams.

Over the past year, interest rates have dropped from 15-18% to rates as low as 8.5%. Chalk this up to more competition in the lending arena; good for you, bad for the lender. You can expect to pay somewhere between 11% or 12%, interest-only on your acquisition/rehab loan when you get started. I always tell my clients to anticipate paying 1% a month, as this is a very manageable rate and it will not break your budget. Interest-only is just that; you will get a bill each month for the funds you borrowed, usually a 12-month fixed rate term broken down in 12 monthly payments. Finish the project in 4 months and your payments stop once you terminate the loan.

Most lenders have a 3-month minimum interest payment requirement, so keep that in mind if you think you're going to blow out each project during the first two months. You are paying for 3 months of interest as a minimum, and try and understand that the lender makes their living managing risk and getting a return on their capital. With the amount of underwriting and the number of fallouts during that process, one or two months of interest on a loan will hardly keep the doors open for a lender. You can try to negotiate the committed payoff length of your loan, and you should if you think you can turn an asset in less than 3-months. I always suggest plan on 4-months or more for a well-orchestrated project.

Points are always part of the conversation, especially as they are paid at the time the loan is funded. They are a fact of life, like breathing, so don't stress over it. The interest rate never creates much of an income for the lender or mitigates the risk. A $100,000 loan at 12% only generates $1,000 a month in income for the lender. You have the money out for 4 months, and the lender makes $4,000 less his underwriting and servicing costs, employment and risk. The added money earned is on the points you pay at the time of funding. The best way to look at points you pay is to divide the points by 12 months. Using the same example as above, on a $100,000 loan you would pay 2 points, or 2%; $2,000, or $500 per month on a four-month project.

Here is my counsel to you.
1. You got your money.
2. Everyone needs to make money in our industry.
3. The cost of money is tax deductible.
4. Borrowing money from a lender is far cheaper than using 100% of your own.

The latter point may be a little confusing, so let me outline an example.

1. Same deal; you find a property to purchase for $106,000, with a rehab budget of $20,000. You borrow 80% of the LTC (Loan to Cost), and 100% of your rehab budget for a total of $100,000. You are going to pay 12% and 2 points on the deal. You have a total of $26,000 of your own money in the deal, the rest is borrowed

2. The ARV (After Repair Value) from the appraiser is $165,000. This is the price you will sell your asset once completed.

If you used your own money, your total investment – forgetting closing costs on the house – is $106,000 for the house and $20,000 for rehab, making a total of $126,000. Selling the property for $165,000 brings a gross profit of $39,000, or a 31% return on invested capital.

Now let's say you borrowed your funds, using only $26,000 of your own money. You paid 2 points, $2,000, and you paid 1% a month for the four months you used the funds, $4,000. Your total out of pocket costs, once again forgetting closing costs, is $32,000. Selling the property for $165,000 brings a gross profit of $39,000, or a 120% return on invested capital. Any questions? Now do you see why the points and rate are not even a conversation?

In today's capital climate, the cheapest expense you have is money. Labor, material and time are far more expensive than the cost of money. Don't buy into the hype and believe you don't need money to get started – of course you do. If you find a deal where you don't need any of your own money, please call me as I want in on it.

The moral of this section is; "you don't need to be entrenched in the acquisition/rehab business to succeed." You don't need to be related to Donald Trump to be successful. What you *do* need is a successful business plan that will attract funding. I have successfully loaned money to bail bondsmen, housewives, doctors, morticians and schoolteachers. They all had the same traits – they were professional, clear to task, and not in possession of grandiose egos. Yes, when your new to the business money will cost you more, Yes, you're not going to get 85% LTC – more like 70% - but you *will* get your money, and your opportunity to partake as an acquisition/rehab professional and begin the journey to millionaire status.

During our conversation on acquisition/rehab I used some terminology you must know. When you buy a property. Lenders are going to lend on the cost of the property – this is called LTC, not the appraised value. Too many times I hear a client tell me, "Tony, I have this sweet deal. I can buy for $85,000 and it will appraise at $175,000." Great, congratulations! And no, I will not lend you $125,000 and you skate with cash in your pocket. You will borrow at the LTC, just like the appraisal will confirm to us what the professional appraiser deems the asset is worth now and after you have rehabbed it.

The second critical term is ARV, or After Repair Value. Lenders will use a percentage, usually 65-75% of the ARV, to confirm your loan amount.

Closing this segment let me share with you a solid philosophy; "always put yourself in the shoes of your lender. Try and understand *why* we ask for the documents and evidence to substantiate your claims, be prepared to explain early, and show everything. I am in the business of lending money, not saying, "no". I can't tell you how many times I have been forced to say that to clients who are angry and frustrated with the process. I only *make* money when I lend you money – when that happens, you're happy and I am smiling, grateful for another successful client. You will take me off your Christmas card list and speak evil of me if I fail you, and I will suffer the failure and ask myself why I took you on as a client to begin with. You and your lender will at some point become one, working in harmony toward your success. This is very different to banks and how they view their clients, which is more akin to sheep being herded into the pen for slaughter.

I have had bad things said to me after *failed* deals, not from clients who walked away at closing with the funds they needed. 100% of my failures have been client driven. The list of reasons is endless, but 95% of the time a failed deal had to do with the client's failure to provide the necessary information, background checks failed, or the deal was flawed and the client could not see it. These matters are on your shoulders as the client, not those of the lender. Own your failures and your effort; that is what capitalism is all about.

12 BRIDGE LOANS

Well, we got through that segment unscathed and you're still reading, so that's a good thing. Most of what I said about acquisition / rehab investing above will pertain to bridge loan financing. There are some subtle differences, but once you get through this segment you can proudly call yourself an expert.

Bridge loans are used for properties that require no rehab work. There you go; now you're an expert. No, really; that is all there is to the conversation. Now to make this a more *interesting* conversation, I will put more effort in my explanation.

Let's say you buy a property from an auction, foreclosure, or an individual who wants to sell on the cheap, or you own a property free and clear and you wish to borrow more than an equity loan. There is no structural work required other than maybe a lick of paint which you will not finance, so basically you buy the property, shine it up and put it on the market or find a rental tenant. *This* is a bridge loan. The first thing you need to understand is that I won't lend you the same ratio on this type of loan as I did when we discussed acquisition/rehab. The best you will get on this type of loan is 75% LTC, maybe as low as 70% LTC.

But why, I hear you ask. It has to do with you putting money in to fix up the property vs. doing nothing but flipping it. In the acquisition/rehab loan you're improving the asset, while with a bridge loan there is no real improvement. The property is as advertised, and we the lender have more risk without improvements.

Now, some lenders won't do rehab funding, my advice is to steer well clear of them. You want to do business with someone like me, I will do both the bridge loan or the acquisition/rehab loan at a lower LTC, but rehab money is always available. One stop shopping saves you time and paperwork. Rehab funding is critical to your success, and will offer you more choices and opportunity for a higher return on capital.

The bridge loan you get will be predicated on the same paperwork and appraisal requirement we discussed earlier. The only factor here is, since there is no rehab budget, the appraisal process is more concerned with the current valuation vs. the ARV. I bet you're thinking that you can now skip the rest of this segment, but before you do, let me share with you this sweet tidbit, starting with the next paragraph. I am going to share a very neat trick that will boost your LTC from 70% to 85%! All by including a simple rehab budget.

Did that capture your attention? Good, because this idea works 100% of the time. If you buy a property that has no rehab needs, and you seek a bridge loan, find some rehab issues – even if they are miniscule. When you present a rehab budget of $10,000 with the house you are purchasing, I will lend you 85% LTC as opposed to the. 70-75% quoted on your bridge loan – assuming you are qualified. This little trick is worth 10% more in funding, so on a $90,000 purchase that is $9,000. Here's the secret; you only need to call $2,500 of the rehab budget prior to closing, leaving the balance of the rehab budget to go unborrowed. We both know you can spend $2,500 very easily on your purchase, and what little work you do will improve your property. Paint, wall sockets, cupboard knobs, carpeting… there is always *something* that will be needed, and you have $2,500 to work with by increasing your bridge loan by 10%.

13 STRUCTURAL DUE DILIGENCE

Even if you're buying a property that appears to need no serious work, an inspection is critical to ensure you're not buying a hidden issue. The physical inspection report vs. a required appraisal examines all that the eye can see, and even some that it cannot. From foundation and roof issues, to the condition of more readily replaceable systems in the house such as HVAC and water heaters, the physical inspection is another critical component of the due diligence process. While few lenders fail to require this added step to their loan procedure, I advocate it 100% of the time as part of our client's investment process. Most investors simply do not properly investigate, anticipate or mitigate the two 'big hit' factors that send borrowers into a financial tailspin: major roof or foundation failures, and age- or weather-related HVAC or plumbing failures. These four, combined with inadequate insurance, account for a disproportionate number of defaults.

When lenders fail to ask about an inspection as part of the underwriting process, they are putting their loan – and your financial success – at risk. Appraisers won't tell you the roof leaks, or the HVAC is not working. They will tell you that the house has a roof, and yes, they saw the water heater. The appraiser's job is to, well, *appraise* the property and render a professional opinion based on comps in the area what your asset is worth, regarding a bridge loan that information reflects the CMV (Current Market Value). A current market valuation appraisal is only going to tell you what the asset is worth in its current state vs. what your property is worth after you make the necessary repairs.

Imagine you bought a property as is, with no inspection. The appraiser has no idea what state of disrepair the roof is in, and confirms in his report that the roof, "appears to be sound." Now you get into what you believe is minor repair work with a contractor, who comes to you with the news that the entire roof needs to be replaced. *Cha-Ching.*

$19,000 for a new roof, and there goes your budget. The lender will not provide additional funding, so you will be forced to either pull the added cash out of your back pocket if you're lucky enough to have those funds, or come to a standstill while the clock ticks on the interest payments while you rush around hoping to find a partner or family member to lend you another $19,000. Even when you *are* successful, you still must deal with the fact the purchase cost $19,000 more you had anticipated, and that comes out of the sale of the asset after it is repaired.

Let's add another wrinkle so you really get the point – this one actually happened to one of my clients. Let's say the same issue exists, except it's mid-December when you learn the truth because the snow on your roof is leaking into one of the bedrooms. You hire a tradesman to replace the roof, but he tells you he cannot do the work until March because of the weather. Now you sit tight for an additional three months as you wait for the snow to subside, while the damage continues and the interest payment mounts. It's the worst possible kind of "snowball" effect.

The moral of this story is to pay for an inspection (the average cost is $250), and make it a contingency to walk away from your purchase contract if the inspection turns up problems. Yes, you *can* have an inspection clause put into the purchase contract that allows you to cancel your deal if the inspection turns up something unexpected and throws your deal over budget, or you can ask the price you offered to be reduced by the repair costs associated with the property.

An inspection is cheap. Too good to be true relates to properties that appear to need little or no rehab work. I can spend weeks discussing deals that appeared to be solid but were poorly reviewed and turned out to be a total loser. I have a graveyard full of clients who failed to complete their rehab work because their project went over budget and they didn't have the necessary funds, or the finished property was going to sell for a loss. Keep this in mind; I don't want your mistakes, I want you to be successful. Foreclosing on a loan is expensive, demoralizing and will ruin our relationship, and what's more I'll be stuck with your turkey.

14 TRANSACTIONAL FUNDING

How Transactional Funding Works

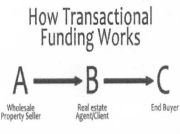

A ➞ B ➞ C

Wholesale Property Seller   Real estate Agent/Client   End Buyer

Another form of very short bridge loan is also known as "transactional funding." This loan is used by wholesalers who are flipping an asset as a middleman, taking a spread between offer price and selling price. It's a double closing on the same day, with a qualified attorney or title company. Try getting your local bank to buy into this strategy, I will buy you dinner!

Speaking to flippers or wholesalers for a moment – you *need* this service to make your project successful. Paying a percentage of your selling price for transactional funding allows you in the game when all you have are the escrow funds needed to go into contract. During a transactional funding deal, the lender comes to the table with the funds necessary to close on the buyer's side and is paid a fee for that service.

As an example: a wholesaler finds a good deal for $125,000 and puts up $1,000 of his own money in an escrow account for the purchase contract. He contacts a buyer and they agree on a price of $137,000 for the property. The wholesaler has a problem; he can't close and pay the seller the balance of $124,000 to sell to his buyer, as that's illegal. So, he comes to a lender who will do a transactional loan of $124,000. Forgetting closing costs, the fee paid to the transactional lender is 1-1.5% of the selling fee, so around $2,055.

Back when I ran a hedge fund we called guys like this "scalpers." There is a place for this group, as they perform a bird-dog service, finding buyers, like you good deals that ordinarily you would never see. If you meet a wholesaler, get to know him and work a deal so he can be paid on the HUD rather than through a transactional funding commitment. The fee to the wholesaler is usually 1-1.5% of the sales price, so the sale of a $100,000 property will cost him $1,500. Keep that in mind when negotiating with the wholesaler.

15 PROPERTY RESEARCH

Because the next topic is sure to be touchy, I am going to unavoidably step on certain toes. Most clients never consider the complete background of the property outside of an inspection, which we covered in the previous segment, prior to purchasing. Let me ask you a question - if you're employing somebody, or about to rent to a tenant, are you doing a background check? If the answer was a yes (which I hope it is), then why not a background check on the property you're about to purchase?

I have saved my clients *so* much heartache and money by doing a background check on properties they bring to me to provide funding. What I do is a courtesy; it has cost me deals, but saved friendships with my clients. Have you ever asked yourself why certain cities are much cheaper than others? You get what you pay for. Sure, you can buy a $35,000 house renting for $600 a month in some metropolitan areas, but, why would you? That house will more than likely be found in a high crime, lower education system area that is going to attract a certain type of tenant. Do you want to work with that type of individual? If you do, that's fine if you have prepared yourself for things like Section 8 housing laws and tenant eviction process, and you plan to set aside money to turn the property and repair the interior if the tenant decides they want your appliances as they skip town. Though this conversation is more focused toward rental properties, it also has viable interest for clients who are looking to buy, rehab and sell. I have seen clients buy an asset for cash in a difficult market without understanding the neighborhood dynamics. They bring the loan to us and after we run an inspection/appraisal, all the copper pipes have been stolen!

If you decide that you have found a great deal that needs work in a difficult neighborhood, make a few calls before you write the check. Ensure that private money lenders will in fact loan you the funds you seek on this deal. Lenders say "no" for many reasons, with neighborhoods and the price of the house two major causes. Many lenders have a minimum of $75,000 for a loan, with some as high as $150,000. I can't tell you how many times clients have called me about the 3 houses they just bought for $50,000 – paid in cash – before they come to me for a bridge loan to cash out their investment. The answer every time is "no," most lenders will not do a blanket loan on several properties, as we lend on each property. In this case, each house is worth $16,500 per property, and no lender is going to be interested in that project. Don't talk yourself into writing a check to pay for your asset if you plan on seeking a bridge loan to recover your investment later. First and foremost, we don't lend at the same LTC as we do on a purchase contract. If I was planning on offering you 80% funding when you presented your purchase contract, I – and most other lenders – are now going to cash you out at 65% LTC. That is a 15% hit on use of capital, just because you convinced yourself you had to pay cash for the asset.

If you're worried about how much time it will take to close a loan, no problem – start on that process first. I discussed earlier how many clients come to us for a loan commitment letter, allowing us to go through an entire underwriting without the property. We then provide a letter of agreement on our loan consideration, and off they go. We can close your house in a week, so surely you can get a close date 14 days from going into contract? This allows you to do a full inspection and appraisal, just to ensure your vision and valuations are correct.

During the initial phase of your review on a property, our company will do an entire review of your targeted asset. Here are my suggestions, based on what we provide our clients who ask us for assistance.

Firstly, do your market research. Start with property management, arranging your financing so you know how much you can borrow and what markets are acceptable, *then* go find an asset. Start with property taxes – the county will tax the asset based on their understanding of the value of the property. If you're offering $89,000 for a little bungalow and the property taxes are based on a valuation of $47,000, you have a problem. You can also find out very easily what the seller paid for the property, and when. If there appears to be a huge spread between the price paid and what the asset is being offered for, there should be a good reason why. If the seller tells you he rehabbed the property before selling, ask him for his rehab budget and scope of work, and price that work out yourself as if you were doing the rehab. Subtract your costings from his offering price, then compare that number to what shows up in the county records; this way, you will know exactly what the sellers profit margin is. Whatever you pay, if it's higher than the current tax rate, your taxes are going up. You can ask the county what the tax rate would be on the asset you intend to purchase, and *that* number needs to be computed into your analysis – not the current tax rate.

You will not find many lenders who are going to finance your 940', 1-bed, 1-bath house. Flipping and buy and hold are two very different avenues, and the valuation studies are roads that lead in diverse directions.

Buying to resell requires you to know the dynamics of the owner-occupied market – things like transportation, parks, school systems, ratio between homeownership and rental properties, comps in the area and crime. How long properties take to sell at a specific price is one of your most serious considerations. If the average property sells in 90 days, as I stated earlier, you will be paying three months of added interest expense on that property while it sits. You need to consider this when you make your offer, not when your contractors and crew clean up and leave the property.

If you plan on renting the property, the same considerations are important to you – especially the ratio between renters and home ownership. If you're buying a property in a neighborhood that has more rentals then home owners, the rent you charge will always be under pressure. I have seen this first hand, especially if there are several property managers involved. Rents fall like a run on the stock market. Remember, the longer your rental sits vacant, those rents lost will never be recovered, and only if you can successfully raise your rents at the next vacancy can you keep up with inflation and recover lost income. Many lenders require lost rent insurance, whereby the insurance company pays you rent if the house sits vacant, ensuring steady cash flow.

Now here is where it gets touchy. If you're buying from a wholesaler, you really need to discover his purchase price. I have a book full of bad deals because the wholesaler bought cheap and laid the deal off to an unsuspecting client at a crazy rate. I will give you one example, recent but relevant. A client came to me with a purchase of a rental property; she was going to pay, $103,000 in Jacksonville, Florida. Her only criteria were that she needed a gross rent return of 1% or better on her investment, so her rental income needed to be $7,800 annually. The client utilized our background and property search service, and what we found surprised her. We discovered that the wholesaler had paid $39,000 for the property two months earlier, spending $20,000 in rehab and placing a low-income tenant in at $650 per month. The property taxes reflected a value of $49,000, while my quick valuation had the property worth $55,000. My client would never have made money from that deal. in fact, it's like buying an over-priced corporate bond with maximum downside risk. I talked my client and myself out of a nice mortgage deal, though I doubt the appraisal would have backed the deal. But the client was spared heartache and an appraisal fee.

Always question wholesalers who tell you they are going to sell you a property 25% below the appraised value, then they show you a tabletop appraisal they got from a buddy. Your offer must be written, "subject to your appraisal," I can honestly say that I have never successfully loaned on this type of deal. The property never appraises at the level the wholesaler has advertised, and the deal turns into a mess.

I will stress this again – *don't be afraid to buy an acquisition/rehab property, or a property that needs some work*. If you do your homework your return on investment will be higher and more rewarding, *and* you will receive the upside appreciation on the property once complete. The real estate industry can create millionaires in a very short period of time – but it can also leave you broke and in serious financial debt with one bad deal. My counsel to you is that every deal needs to be – and can be – successful. Create a checklist of necessary due diligence tasks and adhere to them without fail. The fact is, *we* do our homework, and you're paying us to do extensive reviews, I am not your daddy or best friend, I am your business partner once funds have been lent. Failure occurs when you decide to proceed when red flags are flying.

You have two decisions when buying an asset that you intend to own for the rental income; rental income and property appreciation, or rental income alone. When it comes to selling several years out – maybe you're upgrading your portfolio from SFR properties to duplexes, which is another conversation and a smart idea – buying in weak neighborhoods with low property values is going to tell you there will be little or no appreciation on your property in the future. So, the income you are receiving in rental income is the sole source of revenue for the life of the asset. If your property is appreciating at a rate of 2% per year and inflation is moving at 3% per year or higher, are you making any money on your asset?

I have a client who came to me, so excited. He was buying two houses in Syracuse, New York. "Tony, I can get both for $70,000 and the rental income is $700 per month on each!", he told me. When we did the background checks on the assets, it turns out the client had paid $66,000 and $71,000 for his assets, 11 years ago. The seller was taking a 50% hit in value on each asset. Is that what you really want in your life 10 years from now? The way I talked him out of the purchase was to compare the two houses as if they were two publicly traded stocks. There is a reason those houses had lost 50% of their value – it is related to things such as neighborhoods, work migration and school districts, as well as little things like weather. Can you look forward 10 years and figure out where the asset you're buying is going to be valued? In some ways, yes. Are more people leaving Northern states and moving South? Are property taxes, or personal taxes, higher in the Northeast or the South like Florida, North Carolina, South Carolina, Texas? That is not so tough to figure out, but that is how broadly you need to do your homework to be successful predicting the future.

You're buying rental assets for income, you also are expecting appreciation on your asset. So many investors act like they don't care about the upside of their purchase. Most often, when I ask a client how long they expect to own the property they tell me 30 years. Really – how can one predict that? Do you have a stock portfolio, and do you still own the same stocks you bought 30 years ago? If you do then you own stocks like, Zenith, American Motors, Detroit Steel or Armstrong Rubber. Do you realize 85% of the fortune 500 stocks 30 years ago are gone today? Never plan on owning your rental property for 30 years unless you're in a bulletproof area. America migrates all the time. We moved from the Deep South to the Northeast and Midwest for jobs. We migrated to the West Coast during the great depression, always looking for work. Today we see a different Detroit than even 15 years ago, Illinois is a net loser on their population base, and New York has taxes that can choke any person living on a blue-collar income. My point is this, what you do today, in whatever area you decide to buy rental properties, may not be the right place 10 years from now. Stay on top of your portfolio, and where the properties are located. Don't be afraid to sell and relocate your investment decisions. Your future depends on it.

16 TERM LOANS

Ah yes, the final steps toward the beginning of a successful buy and hold strategy. Term loans are used by clients who are keeping the asset, putting a tenant in place and enjoying long term positive cash flow – and, we hope, upside appreciation. We have term loan discussions every day with clients, from newly acquired assets to existing properties held, and the client is seeking a cash out – refinance mortgage. This is where conventional and non-conventional, or "Outside Dodd Frank", loans become more of a conversation. I will give you all the facts here to assist you with realty vs. market myths.

First things first; there are Federal loan programs in your area that will lend to qualified borrowers on rental properties at very low rates. Freddie and Fannie are the two government programs that you should investigate to see if you qualify. For the most part, you will be restricted to nine assets in your name, and another nine assets for your spouse (though this number changes all the time) –assuming you qualify to borrow in the program. The one key component to knowing if you're qualified is whether you have W2 income and a solid credit score. Some local banks will lend on rental properties as well, but again W2 income and a credit score are the two primary considerations when reviewing your purchase. Conventional banks will lend based on the individual's credit worthiness, while private money lends on the asset valuation.

Now that we have conventional mortgage financing out of the way, we can focus on private mortgage financing. This is a huge market, and growing every year. Private money, or "outside Dodd Frank, is the likely place you will find yourself looking for a 30-year mortgage. But after reading the balance of this chapter, you will learn the various choices and what to expect.

The first thing you need to learn is a little discussed term, *Red Lining*. Conventional finance forbids federal banks from deeming a city or neighborhood un-lendable. If you have a property in the middle of the worst ghetto in America and you are qualified, a loan *must* be provided.

On the other hand, private mortgage funding can say, *no* for any arbitrary condition it chooses to apply. These parameters are changing all the time, however. For instance, distance from a major metropolitan area, the metro area itself, property valuation, DSCR number (more on that later), the price you're paying, the size of the house, your mother's middle name... (that one was a joke – kind of). The point is, whatever reason we decide to use to say *no* to you is our prerogative and legal right. Once again, this is where you get yourself preapproved for both market and price.

Together, let's go over all the criteria you'll need to make your 30-year mortgage loan a success, and what it takes to comply with underwriting. Everything we discussed earlier will apply here as well, so if you blew through the terms and conditions I discussed during the acquisition/rehab and bridge segments you'll need to grab another cup of coffee and review what was earlier discussed. Even if you're a seasoned investor, this section is going to be a good review. As new lenders come into the market, the rates, strategies, markets and necessary documents change on a regular basis. My team spends countless hours reviewing the multitude of changes that come at us every day, and with regard to the 30-year mortgage markets, information is the key to success.

The first understanding you need to embrace is that *you will not close a term loan in less than 30 days*. I don't care who is telling you anything different – the facts are clear regarding term loans, and you will need to allow 30-45 days for success. If you ever went through the mortgage process on your own home, you'll remember you spent at least 45 days before making that mortgage a reality. This is not very different, and the primary reason is that lenders in the private markets sell every loan we write.

In the loan industry, there are loan originators – which is what my company is – and there are brokers who shop your mortgage to originators. There are servicing companies who provide you your payment book and to whom you send your payment, and finally there is a growing market of loan buyers. These institutions will buy a written loan for the coupon income provided by your interest rate to *earn* the income. The reason it appears to be a slow process is because every loan written must meet a higher standard; that of the institution who will buy that loan from the loan originator. We all serve a greater master, and you will need to meet that loan criteria. Once you understand this process, the mortgage loan you seek will make sense, and we will embrace each other as though we are in this loan effort together and stop fighting the need to comply.

Private money loans are packaged into portfolios and sold to hedge funds, insurance companies or even commercial banks, who will buy a loan portfolios for the income. Any institutions looking for stable income derived from mortgage income are buyers. Today, unlike 2008 during the great real estate scam from the CDO markets, term loans are very efficient, safe and void of the scandal that plagued the real estate industry during those tumultuous times.

When you apply for a private money mortgage, you will be asked to provide a variety of documents, tax returns and bank statements. We will run a credit report, an appraisal will be performed, and if you're buying the property, a copy of your purchase contract, past-experience owning rental properties will be required. Without experience you will be asked to secure a property manager; unlike conventional financing, whereby the mortgage is put into your name, private money mortgages lend into an LLC or corporation. Choose a non-taxable state (Delaware, Nevada, Florida or Texas, for instance, as this way you're not paying state income taxes on your rental income. It doesn't matter if your Delaware LLC owns property in South Carolina – you don't need to have an LLC in the state you're buying in, but you will need that entity first.

You will provide a copy of your operating agreement for the LLC, or similar documents for your corporation. Be sure you can produce a copy of the letter of good standing which every state provides, as this assures the lender that your LLC or corporation is up to date with all required filings, as well as any taxes owned. Lenders will expect proper identification from yourself so we know who we're doing business with. You'll notice that this is pretty much the same information you were asked to provide when you sought an acquisition/rehab loan or bridge loan. What you *won't* have to do is the mountain of paperwork required when applying for a conventional loan. Private money mortgage loans rely on the asset valuation, whereas conventional mortgage loans rely on your W2 income.

Here is why working with a Company like mine makes so much sense. From acquisition/rehab funding to a term loan, *we do it all for you*. Like going to Catholic School, which I did from Grade One through High School all under the same roof, that is our business model. The biggest difference is that we don't sell acquisition/rehab loans; they are serviced in-house, but 100% of term loans are sold. Here is the biggest reason to stick with one lender who will transition from an acquisition/rehab loan to a term loan – *you pay no added points*. When you go to Lender A for the acquisition/rehab loan you paid points; now, you seek a 30-year term loan guess what you're paying again – points. We give you a free ride.

There are two numbers you need to be aware of, and when each come into play. When you're buying a property, the lender is going to give you a mortgage based on the price you are paying for the property, LTC (Loan to Cost). If, on the other hand, you have owned the property for an extended amount of time, then the loan will be made on the LTV (Loan to Value). This is based on an appraisal. Now, what is that extended period of time? This is a constant debate within the mortgage industry.

Back during the real estate crash of 2008-10, there was a great scam perpetrated on the banking system and Federal Government. A property would be purchased for $35,000, but then the buyer would find a buddy who worked as an appraiser and increase that number to $65,000. The bank would lend some crazy number, such as 90% of the appraised value. Well, *that* broke our economy, as you might recall. Thousands of properties were valued at their bogus appraised value and millions of dollars were swindled from the banking system. Every bank that wrote mortgages suffered, and many closed their doors.

Today we have a term used, *seasoning*, which describes the length of time you have owned the property. That number among private lenders averages about five to six months. Now, because Freddie and Fannie and other government loan programs haven't learned their lesson, you can still get a loan based on the appraised value even if you bought the property 30 days ago.

If the property has been held for more than five months, the appraised value (LTV) will be used for a cash-out refinance mortgage; the amount you can pull will be 65-70% of the appraised value. When you buy the property, and apply for the mortgage, you will be provided with a 75- 80% LTC.

I advise my clients that have purchased a property and rehabbed it with the intention of keeping the asset as a rental to remain on the acquisition/rehab loan we provided them for an additional five months. During that time, they will secure a tenant and collect rent for this period and guess what – they are *seasoning* the asset. Now we go for their 30-year mortgage on a cash-out basis, but the LTV will be used rather than LTC.

Example: You purchase a property with rehab included for $120,000, and you put a tenant into the house paying $1,350 per month. Five months later, when the property is appraised during the mortgage process, it comes in at $165,000. You will get a mortgage for $107,250.00, recovering almost 90% of your original investment. Your monthly mortgage payment would be $715 based on a 30 year, 7% mortgage. Estimating taxes and insurance of $290 per month, your net annual income is, $4,140. Your net investment into the property after the cash-out refi mortgage is $12,500, giving you a net return on investment of – drum roll, please – better than 33% per year. And best of all, you have $100,000 in your pocket to do it again.

Same example, but let's imagine that this time you are buying the same property, already rehabbed, from a wholesaler. Let's say the wholesaler is a nice guy, so he is giving you the property at $145,000, which is $20,000 below appraised value. We both know his price would be closer to the appraised value of $165,000, but for example's sake we will make him a very generous guy.

You will get your mortgage on the purchase price LTC, and the appraisal will be used to confirm the LTV, ensuring the numbers are within the correct range. 75% of a $145,000 down payment would be $36,250, and your mortgage payment would be $723.52. Taxes and insurance would remain the same, $290, as would the rental income. Your net return on investment would be 11% per year.

The best LTC on a 30-year mortgage is usually 75-80%. Again, we need you to be involved financially - it makes us sleep better at night. So, you can expect to have a down payment available of 25%, plus your closing costs. 80% LTC mortgages are available, but understand that you will pay for that extra bump with a higher interest rate – usually 50 basis points.

Your credit score rules during the term loan process. Yes, you can get a term loan with a credit score of 580, but high scores bring lower rates – as does lower LTCs. Your rate will go down as you move from 75% LTC to 60% LTC, and keep this in mind if you're doing a cash-out refi. If you have a house with no mortgage expect, no better than a 65% LTV as we discussed earlier, provided you have held the asset longer than five months. Now let's get into a very important number; the number that will control your LTV when you're doing a cash-out refi or putting a mortgage on a rental property. What is your DSCR Number?

17 DSCR

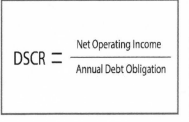

$$DSCR = \frac{\text{Net Operating Income}}{\text{Annual Debt Obligation}}$$

DSCR, which stands for Debt Service Coverage Ratio, is the ratio of cash available for debt servicing of Principal, Interest, Taxes and Insurance – also known as PITI. We are going to take your property taxes, insurance coverage, principal and interest payment (once the loan is written) vs. your rental income. The lowest DSCR number most lenders can loan against is 1.2, and the higher your number the more LTV you can receive.

Example: Your rental income is: $1,100 a month, while you pay $129 a month for taxes and $68 a month for insurance. We will also consider any HOA (Home Owners Association Dues) if they apply. Now the loan you seek is $102,000, the interest rate is 7%, and it's a 30-year amortized loan. Your mortgage payment would be $672 per month. Now we have the facts lets figure out your DSCR number.

Debt Service Coverage Ratio (DSCR) = <u>Net Operating Income</u>
Or in other words: Total Debt Service

Net operating income is: <u>rent – taxes and insurance</u> = $903.00
Debt Service (P&I)   = $672.00

Your DSCR number for this example is: 1.34

If your number goes up toward 1.5 this is very good – the higher you go, whoopee, we love you like a step-child. Alas, as your number moves toward 1.2, your interest rate won't go higher but your LTV drops. This is to ensure that your income can cover your PITI payments. When your DSCR number goes below 1.2, it's *sayonara baby*.

Do you feel smarter? Are you seeing now why the need to buy right and in the right area is critical to a successful term loan?

When you're involved with refinancing a property you own outright without a mortgage, the appraisal is kind of an afterthought. You're clear as to your DSCR number, and have a close understanding of the value of your property. But, when you're buying the asset and going directly to a term loan – for instance, you found a wholesaler who has a tenant ready asset – you need to do your homework. This deal can be sticky if you don't have your basic facts before you submit, like the actual rent you can charge vs. what the wholesaler is telling you.

Let's move off the term loan topic for a moment and talk strategy. The first thing to understand when you buy a fully renovated rental property is that the wholesaler is going to absorb all your equity. You're paying retail plus, hoping the appraisal doesn't let you down. I am always amazed when I hear investors are buying these assets for all cash – why would anyone do that? Furthermore, are they ordering an independent appraisal to ensure they are buying value? It is like paying over par for a corporate or municipal bond. Par is $1,000 on any bond, when you pay $1,200 for that bond two things happen; your yield dropped to represent the coupon, and you will never see the $200 you overpaid again. Buying a rental property from a wholesaler is the same thing; you are paying no better than the appraised value for the asset. That wholesaler bought it much cheaper, did some cosmetic rehab, and flipped it to you at the market value, a premium to his cost of goods and rehab.

All the upside is gone for many years, just like a premium corporate bond. You'll see no equity, just a yield on money. So here is my question to you –what happens if you need to sell this asset in a down market? Yep, you'll lose money and the income you realized from rental is gone to offset the loss you took when selling the asset. The moral of the story is to not buy another person's hard work. Put your team together, and do it yourself. Hold on to that equity, as you'll need it one day. I still hear stories about big players in the real estate market who lost everything in 2008. When you pay full price for a rental property you are setting yourself up for that same result, and please don't repeat the most often quoted statement in the investment community – *"things are different now! That won't happen to me."*

Remember the issue that plagued clients who overpaid for their acquisition during their acquisition/rehab project? The property you're buying as a rental will have similar issues. As I mentioned earlier, you need to expect no better than 75% LTC on your mortgage. During the appraisal process, you will also be appraised on your rental lease. This is called a 1007 appraisal.

The 1007 appraisal will validate your lease and lease assumptions. For instance, you have a property and the rent you're asking is $1,450 per month, but the average market rent for your area is $1,175. This is going to be a problem for you. You're going to ask me, *"why should I be penalized if I found someone who will actually pay more for my rental?"* or tell me, *"I really went all out on the rehab, and therefore I get more rental income."*

Believe it or not, the appraiser *will* penalize you, and lenders are going to accept the lower rental income shown by the appraiser when we perform our analysis. Though you have been successful today with a higher paying tenant, what happens when they move out? Remember, the average market rent in your area is $1,175. What happens during this next go around, when you can't find a tenant to pay the higher market price you're asking? Now your rental sits for an extended period while you wait for that one perfect tenant. Both you and your property manager begin to reduce the rent until someone bites, usually when you drop to around the average market rent for your area. I have seen this problem time and again, and keep in mind that if your rental sits vacant for three months, that rent loss will never be made up. That money is gone forever, but your mortgage payments continue unchanged. For this reason, most lenders require rental insurance while your property sits vacant. Rent is paid through your policy during this vacant period, and therefore we accept the lower rent recommendation on your 1007 when computing your DSCR number.

There are two morals to this segment on 1007s. Firstly, make sure that you know the average rent for your market. – we provide that service to our clients who ask for such assistance. More importantly, however, never, *never* over-rehab the property you intend to rent. I keep my wife away from properties we intend to hold and rent because she fancies herself as an interior designer. Add a little granite here and a new appliance there, and before you know it the budget is way out of whack and the ROI is upside down. You must be savvy when it comes to the right amount of rehab for rental properties. One of our keys is to go view the competition, act like a rental tenant and go walk around the houses with a property manager, this gives you good insight as to the type and amount of rehab you need to do, and the market rents in your area.

When you buy a property without a tenant, this becomes a challenge for the lender. Some will not even *make* a term loan until you have a tenant. I always recommend our clients get a good lease written and ready even though the property is not yet yours; you can hire a property manager, secure the lease and the expected rental income prior to the application process, or if buying from a wholesaler, make sure a tenant is lodged in the property prior to closing, you can require this effort as part of the contract.

A quick comment on second liens – any lender who is writing a term loan on your property will never tolerate them. Any hint that you're borrowing your down payment will end the mortgage effort.

18 TERM LOAN DOCUMENTATION

If the term loan you're seeking is for a new acquisition the same documentation will be in play as the prior lending programs. Private lending programs require you to buy your property in an LLC or corporation. The operating agreement, and letter of good standing from the State you filed in, will be expected from the lender. Two months of bank statements, which show the funding necessary to make your down payment as well as other carry costs, should be evident – as should a personal financial statement, proper I.D, and a letter stating you do not intend to occupy the property. You will produce the purchase contract (or your HUD if you paid cash for the asset) at an earlier date. You'll need a copy of your lease, even if you don't have a tenant, and of course an outline of any past rentals you have bought. If this is your first property it's not a problem, but most lenders will expect you to provide the name of your property manager. If you intend on managing your properties yourself and this is your first one, I suggest – and most lenders will *insist* – that you hire a property manager.

You can't borrow your down payment. Funds can be gifted, but you need to show evidence of this event. Funds that are transferred into your account, showing large deposits prior to the loan, will result in you being asked to show the source of those funds. This would include the bank statements where that money came from. There is a law called anti-money laundering, and lenders must comply with the government when it comes to large deposits.

19 OUTSIDE DODD FRANK LENDING

 There are great lending programs with rates more competitive than private money mortgages in every State. These mortgages are called Outside Dodd Frank Lending. I call these quasi-conventional mortgages, as they're a hybrid that falls between conventional and private money. Rates can be more than 1% lower than private money mortgages, but they do require more paperwork that can be taxing for some.

These mortgages are always my first choice for our clients, providing they qualify. W2 income is not necessary, but if you have it you're in the wheelhouse. Bank statements for the previous 12 or 24 months, used mainly by self-employed individuals, can replace W2 income. The loan is written in your name just like a conventional mortgage, but you can transfer the property to an LLC upon closing. Rates usually start very low, much like conventional mortgages, then basis points are added for various issues. Some of these issues include the amount of the loan, your credit score, what program you are filing under, rental or second home and W2 income vs. 12 or 24-month bank statements. You can also buy down your rate, which is not an option with private money mortgages.

Let's say you have been offered a rate of 6.5% and you speak with your lender about lowering the rate to 6%. The standard adjust will cost you 1% on the purchase price for .05% of a lowered rate. The house you are purchasing as a rental is $185,000, and the buy down will cost you, $1,850.

The difference of .05% calculation in your monthly mortgage payment is $1,169.33 vs. $1,109.17. Your monthly saving is $60.16, which makes $721.92 annually. You spent $1,850, so divide this by the monthly savings of $60.16 and you will see that it takes 31 months to break even. However, you still have 28 years on your mortgage, so the total saving over 360 months is $21,657.

This is the point you need to ask yourself a serious question – how long do I plan on owning this rental property? If longer than 30 months, this could be a good strategy. Less than 30 months, the answer is obvious.

Another very important issue to contend with are mortgage brokers who are unlicensed, and therefore not regulated. These brokers put out their shingle, call themselves a mortgage broker, and look for clients to assist. Nothing wrong with this group who do provide a good service, but these brokers are not able to access any mortgage programs for you other than private money mortgage lenders. The rate you're offered will always be higher, and the points you pay will double, because both the lender and the mortgage broker are going to charge points.

Investment real estate vs. owner occupied real estate has very clear regulation differences. A broker who sells owner occupied mortgages is licensed in the States they work within. On the other hand, there are only a handful of States that require a mortgage broker to be licensed in order to facilitate an investor with their mortgage needs.

The licensing organization is the NMLS. Every mortgage broker with an NMLS number is, in fact, able to bring you to the promised land of lower rates. This is an easy question for you to ask the mortgage broker you're speaking with; "what is your NMLS number, please?" You'll either hear a deafening silence, or his number will be shared immediately. Now you have a choice to make – do you want the Full Monty, or just the private money lending programs that would be available to you?

Our Company is licensed with the NMLS, but we will not undertake financing of owner occupied properties. Our only focus is on investment real estate. There are lenders who *do* cover owner occupied properties, but will not migrate toward investment real estate. You need to learn who will and won't work with your investment program.

During the underwriting process, most mortgage deals fail due to lower than expected credit scores, late mortgage payment history, lack of necessary capital and the appraisal. Private failed deals pertain to poor credit or late payment issues.

Private lenders will not bend below 620, most are higher. I will accept a 620 and lower credit score, providing there are no serious glaring issues with the credit report. "Outside Dodd Frank" programs offered by licensed brokers can accommodate credit scores below 600.

When we run your credit, the first understanding you must grasp, is that we don't use the same report you get from Credit Karma, or one of the other free programs. Our credit report focuses on past and current mortgage liability, and your ability to pay on time. If you have a history of late mortgage payments, there is not much I or any other lender can do for you. Too many credit pulls will increase your rate because your credit score drops like a rock. My advice is to avoid shopping lenders and allowing each to begin the underwriting process, as that would include pulling your credit, until you're closer to a deal. You can inform the lender not to pull your credit until you have committed to a loan that makes sense for your property. We never pull credit until well after a term loan term sheet has been issued, and we agree on the terms and conditions of your mortgage. Your only questions to any lender should be their rate, terms and LTV. Not many lenders offer the variety of loans as <u>Real Estate Lender USA</u>, from conventional and semi-conventional to private money term mortgages. You need to understand all the various products currently offered; knowledge is king.

So, what kind of term mortgage can you expect to have offered? ARM products are the most popular, offering the lowest rates. 3/1 – 5/1 - 7/1 are the three most common ARM products offered. 30-year fixed mortgages are possible, but you will pay for the opportunity – usually .05-1% higher than the 7/1 ARM. Keep in mind that rates will always be higher in the private money mortgage market compared to conventional or quasi-conventional lending. However, you will also have less paperwork with a private mortgage lender than any other program.

Those lenders offering no document loans are relying on your fear of paperwork, as well as the fear of the unknown at a very stiff price – much higher interest rates. My advice is to stay away from these lenders; they are *not* offering you what you think you're hearing or reading about.

If you have serious glaring issues with credit or capital, I advise you to address these issues first before trying to frustrate yourself with the effort of borrowing money. Lenders *want* to lend money. Unlike banks, who will offer a lot of lip service but little actual service, private money lenders are in the business of lending capital so they can make a living. I always tell our clients that lending them as much money as possible with as little risk as possible is my job. I don't make anything by saying no.

The beauty of our industry is how there are so many ways to make money, and so many willing, well-qualified partners. I have put more credit risk investors together with qualified people, creating successful business partnerships and lending to the new entity, than I can remember.

20 MYTHS AND FALSEHOODS ABOUT THE LENDING INDUSTRY (AKA "BUT I WAS TOLD...")

There is a lot of hype in our industry. You can watch rehabbers on TV doing one fabulous deal after another, then you hear about that rehab team showing up in your town for a real estate seminar. They are going to share their alleged insider secrets, and you too can make big money.

The big day arrives, and you head to the local hotel with a pad of paper and pen to write down the wonderful insight that will be shared by your favorite TV personality. Wait, who is that bald headed guy on the stage? And so, the nonsense begins.

No, you won't learn any insights on how the real estate industry works or how you can make a fortune buying property way under value, rehab and then "flip" the asset for thousands of dollars of profit. You will be given the opportunity to write a check for several thousand dollars, come back in a couple weeks and spend the entire weekend listing to more nonsense about how the industry works and how you fit in. You'll walk away with a notebook full of worthless information, and still have no clue how to get started. But wait! You can write *another* check to attend a very secret, insiders-only seminar held in another city. Naturally you'll have to travel there at your own expense, but you'll finally climb the mountaintop with a select group and be shown behind the curtain.

These events are just plain nonsense. Most are run by large corporations that have never completed a single acquisition/rehab deal in their lives. They hire talking heads that are very good at selling, but very poor at real content. They're *great* at cashing your check, though.

Myths and Fiction

Every industry suffers from myths; folklore notions that cloud reality and judgment. I am going to address the most egregious misconceptions about our industry.

Myth #1 You will be able to borrow money without producing any information about yourself.

Facts: "No doc" loans are a myth. No income, no asset, and no employment verification loans were a primary reason we had the real estate meltdown in 2008. You might not have to provide tax returns, but expect to provide a financial statement, bank records and proof you have the necessary capital to complete the transaction. If you find a lender who will give you a loan with very little information other than a bank statement… now *this* you can call "hard money." It will be very expensive, very restrictive, and very short term. Your life is going to become very hard going this route.

Myth #2 An appraisal or BPO is not necessary. You're going to be screwed on the appraisal fees, and most appraisals are bogus anyway.

Facts: There are two forms of professional property evaluation procedures. Your property is going to undergo one of them. Either an appraisal or BPO (Broker Professional Opinion) will be performed on the asset prior to a loan closing.

Individuals who have received formal training and are licensed to evaluate your asset complete appraisals. They have downside risk if they fail to do their job correctly, because their licensing agency can drop the hammer on them. A BPO is a professional in the real estate industry providing his opinion based on standard a review process to render a valuation. If your appraisal or BPO comes in low, it will change your entire computation. I will lend on a 70% of ARV, which protects me from a bad deal. Here is an example:

You're rolling the dice when you rely on a BPO more so than an appraisal. Many clients will jump at the chance for a cheap BPO, usually $125 vs. an appraisal at $450. Don't come into this side of the business with a cheapskate mentality; insist on the appraisal every time if you're given the choice. I have had deals broken because the appraisal failed to certify the client's valuation, but I have had more deals break because of a faulty BPO.

I know it hurts when an appraisal comes in below what you believed the property was worth, and for what it's worth I'm sorry when that happens. Recently I was building duplexes in Tulsa, Oklahoma, and the lending bank was certain the appraised value was $225,000 per duplex, I was excited and began building. The first two were completed and I sold them for $225,000 with a tenant. The appraisals then came back from the clients lending bank at $210,000! Why? Because the comps for duplexes were 32 miles away, there were no comps in our neighborhood with whom to compare values. Ouch, that was a painful one. So, I had to drop my price to $210,000, take a $30,000 hit, and move on. This is the fact of life in our world; I have learned to embrace the appraisal as my truth provider. Yes, from time to time your opinion and that of the appraiser is off, but keep in mind they are licensed and trained for the appraisal process and you're not.

Myth #3   I can borrow money for my acquisition/rehab project, even if I have a poor credit score.

Facts: No, that is not going to happen. Your credit score is a primary factor when it comes to loan rates, and the amount you can borrow. You *must* protect your credit score. It is worth more in our business than any other factor, including capital.

Private money lenders can tolerate past bankruptcies if they have been discharged, bad credit card issues that are in the past, even foreclosures – but we will not, let me repeat myself, *we will not,* tolerate late mortgage payments of any kind. More deals are killed because the client can't pay their mortgage or mortgages on time.

Stand in my shoes for a moment. If a client is late making mortgage payments, are they going to pay *me* on time? Now you see the problem, and I stay away from it. I always recommend to my clients to subscribe to a credit-reporting program that will not ding your score when you make an inquiry. Refute everything if something comes up late, and protect your score as though it was your only child. Be prepared to explain the issues before you get into the process so there are no surprises later. I have a sympathetic ear, but I am not a miracle worker. Figure 45 days to clean up a credit report, and get started now – don't wait until you need money for a great deal. The deal will not save your credit risk, or your background check. Yes, we run background checks for those of you who are hiding and using an alias.

If your credit score is below 620 (and remember that we use the mid score), you will have issues borrowing funds. Sure, you can get a mortgage on a house with that score, but we're not talking conventional mortgages here, are we?

Several benchmarks drive an interest rate, and the key one is credit score. The higher your number, we consider you a better risk. This holds true with new borrowers, by the way; if you want to impress me on your first loan request, come in with a 700+ credit score. You will have me smiling and feeling good about working with you.

I have lent to felons, but they were smart enough to step up and discuss the issues on the first call. If you have a felony, it will depend on the type. Get it out in the open, and when it happened. Here is fact of life; if you used to rob banks or have been convicted of financial fraud, a loan will not happen. There are some hard stops, and this is one of them.

I am a lender, not a loan counselor. I don't solve problems, but I know how to correct issues. My counsel to you is to be open, honest and treat your lender like your best friend. This is how we can get through issues, or I will give you advice on how to get around the issue yourself. I, like most good lenders who care, know all the ways to turn a bad situation into a good deal for both client and lender.

Myth #4 Getting a bunch of credit cards is the right way to finance your project.

Facts: I sat in a seminar once and the guy teaching pulled out a stack of credit cards. There had to be twenty or thirty cards, and he said with a straight face that, "the secret to success in this business is having a lot of credit cards that you then use to "fix and flip" properties." This is pure nonsense. Credit card interest rates are the highest rates in the country, sometimes as high as 24%. Why would you want to pay that type of rate when I would loan a new investor money at 12%? If you can qualify for a credit card, the chances are good that you can get an acquisition/rehab loan.

Trying to manage multiple card payments, run a rehab operation *and* keep going to your day job would be like childbirth. You will ruin your credit beyond repair, you might never finish the project, and you'll find yourself in a world of debt and destruction. You'll get hit on your credit score when you overuse your credit cards and, you get hit on your credit score when you don't use them at all. Go figure.

Myth #5 "I don't have a lot of money in the bank but I can borrow the down payment from my equity line of credit or my best friend."

Facts: This, my friends, is leverage – and lenders will not tolerate this. What you're doing is borrowing 100% of the investment. Earlier I told you that we want you to have a stake in your investment.

When we lend money, we are taking a first lien on the asset. We will not allow a second, third or even a promissory note. When your money is at risk in front of the lender, we are happy. You will not encumber that asset with any other debt. Any lender will shut down the loan if we sniff another loan is in play to make the deal work. I have seen so many shenanigans from clients that think they are smart until we dig into their background and banking. We must follow federal anti-money laundering regulations or risk jail time, and trust me, I am not going to the big house so that you can buy a sweet rehab deal in Camden, New Jersey. Therefore, we ask for at least two months of bank statements. It not only shows us your liquidity, but also large deposits over $10,000. You will be asked to show the origination of those funds every time, so expect it and provide the information when asked. Don't whine and stamp your feet; *just show me*. I need to know where those funds came from, and who sent the wire or made the deposit on your behalf. If you can't produce that information, then see ya later, we're done.

If you don't have the money and your best friend does, make him a partner. Now we're all on the same page, and I have a smile on my face once again.

Myth #6 Lenders will finance my $200,000 property *and* $150,000 rehab.

Facts: This isn't just a "*no*" – this is a "*hell no.*" Outside of the Left Coast, where crazy real estate deals reside, no lender is interested in financing your purchase that includes an expensive rehab. Here, again, you need to walk in my shoes. I make money by lending money and taking as little risk as possible on your deal. A $200,000 house with a rehab budget equal to 75% of the purchase price is an investment with huge risk all over it. You need to figure no better than 50% of the purchase price is a qualified rehab budget. Spend $200K on the property, and we will consider a $100K rehab budget.

Myth #7 "My wholesaler told me I can put a mortgage on the property I am buying from him based on the appraised values once I buy it from him."

Facts: This is an absolute fabrication. If you're buying through a wholesaler, you will be lent money based on cost and ARV will support that number. Just like I discussed earlier, you will never get an acquisition/rehab, bridge loan or a 30-year mortgage based on the appraised value of the property if you have no seasoning.

Myth #8 You will find a loan for your $20,000 acquisition and $15,000 rehab project.

Facts: Most likely, this is not going to happen. Lenders have established minimums on what they will lend. Many new investors think they will "cut their teeth" on a cheap property and low rehab budget to learn the industry, but this is a huge mistake if you plan on borrowing funds to do your next transaction. Know the lending parameters and stay within their boundaries. All cash out of your pocket, no problem, go for it.

There are way too many silly notions about borrowing funds for me to put here. I have covered what I feel are critical myths that need to be discussed so you can appear to be a professional investor, and not somebody who is dipping their toe in the water of real estate. Lenders want to know you're serious about your project, and that there is no risk of you walking away from it.

21 TERMINOLOGY

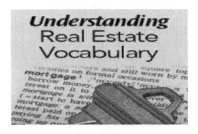

Below are terms you should learn and be able to use in normal conversation with lenders. This knowledge will allow you to sound professional and not have the look of a deer in the headlights when you're having a discussion.

ARM (Adjustable Rate Mortgage) – An adjustable rate mortgage is a loan with an interest rate that fluctuates. The initial interest rate of the ARM will likely be lower than many fixed rate mortgages, but this only lasts for a certain amount of time. After this introductory fixed-rate period, your monthly payments will increase or decrease according to the interest rate, which is tied to an adjustment index. The most popular ARM product in our industry is a 7/1 ARM; stay away from anything less.

ARM's come with caps and ceilings that put limits on the increase of interest rates over the life of the loan. This helps prevent your monthly payments from getting too high, and will help to look past the uncertainty that comes with ARMs.

PROS:

- When interest rates fall, you don't have to go through the hassle of refinancing and paying the fees that go with it. Instead, your monthly payments adjust automatically to reflect the lower rates.

- The lower introductory rates mean your payments for the first few months are going to be small. Take advantage of this time to save and invest the extra cash for a larger return.

CONS:

- Budgeting is not easy. Having to work around fluctuating monthly payments makes it difficult to create a household spending plan and savings.

- Refinancing an adjustable rate mortgage is pricey. If you choose to switch to a fixed rate mortgage, you may end up spending more money than what you would have, sticking with rising interest rates.

Annual Percentage Rate – The APR is the rate of interest that will be paid back to the mortgage lender. The rate can either be a fixed rate or adjustable rate.

Amortization – The amortization of the loan is a schedule on how the loan is intended to be repaid. For example, a typical amortization schedule for a 30-year loan will include the amount borrowed, interest rate paid and term. The result will be a month breakdown of how much interest you pay, and how much is paid on the amount borrowed.

Appraisal – This is conducted by a professional appraiser who will look at a property and give an estimated value based on physical inspection and comparable houses that have been sold in recent times within the area of your investment.

Balloon Payment – A larger-than-usual payment to be made usually at the end of a mortgage term or an amortization loan is called a balloon payment. Lenders can lower interest rates and monthly payments by placing a large lump sum final payment on your mortgage. My advice? This is what destroyed most investors in 2008. You have a balloon payment due, but no lender will do a take out. What then?

Cash-Out Refinance – Normally, a mortgage refinance is when an investor gets a new loan in order to take advantage of lower interest rates. A cash-out refinance, on the other hand, replaces the original loan with a larger mortgage payment in return for immediate cash. Used successfully by investors to drain their equity and reinvest. Your DSCR number will dictate the amount you can pull from your property.

Closing Costs – There are several fees that are charged by those involved in a mortgage that need to be paid, called the closing costs. Depending on your contract and the type of fee, these costs are paid by you or the seller, but never the lender in a private money transaction.

Construction Mortgage – when a person is having a home-built, they will typically have a construction mortgage. With a construction mortgage, the lender will advance money based on the construction schedule of the builder. When the home is finished, the mortgage will convert into a permanent mortgage.

Debt-to-Income Ratio – Lenders look at several ratios and financial data to determine if the borrowers can repay their loan. One such ratio is the debt-to-income ratio. In this calculation, the lender compares the monthly payments, including the new mortgage, and compares it to monthly income. The income figure is divided into the expense figure, and the result is displayed as a percentage. The higher the percentage, the riskier the loan is for the lender.

Down Payment – The down payment is a percentage of the purchase price and the initial upfront payment made when buying property. The down payment is essentially seen as your investment in the mortgage, since you stand to lose it if you default on the monthly payments that come after. A standard 30-year mortgage down payment is 75% of purchase price.

Equity – The difference between the value of the home and the mortgage loan is called equity. Over time, as the value of the home increases and the amount of the loan decreases, the equity of the home generally increases.

Earnest Money (Earnest Money Deposit) – Earnest Money is paid by the buyer to confirm that he or she is serious about purchasing from the seller. This deposit becomes part of the down payment and closing costs once the deal is finalized. However, if you don't close on the property, it is not guaranteed that you will be reimbursed for the deposit. Ensure you are protected by a simple clause that will allow your earnest money to be returned if a closing is not consummated.

Escrow – At the closing of the mortgage, the borrowers are generally required to set aside a percentage of yearly taxes to be held by the lender. On a monthly basis, the lender will also collect additional money to be used to pay the taxes on the home. This escrow account is maintained by the lender, who is responsible for sending the tax bills on a regular basis.

FICO Score (Fair Isaac Corporation) – Your FICO score is a number that represents your creditworthiness. One of the most widely accepted credit scores, this number comes from an algorithm that was developed by Fair, Isaac and Company (now called FICO). FICO is a data analytics company that uses consumer credit files collected from different credit bureaus to compute a credit score.

FICO obtains credit reports from three major credit bureaus: Equifax, Experian and Trans Union. The score is derived by applying data from credit reports to a formula. Although the exact formula used by FICO is confidential, we know the different components to it; the amount of your overall debt, your history of making payments on time, the length of your credit history, the number of times your credit has been pulled, and the types of credit used.

Your FICO score is one of the credit scores that may be seen by lenders in order to determine how likely you are to make timely payments on your mortgage. Therefore, it's important to know how low or high it is. The higher the score, the better your chances are of getting a lower interest rate on your mortgage.

Fixed Rate Mortgage – This is a mortgage where the interest rate and the term of the loan is negotiated and set for the life of the loan. The terms of fixed rate mortgages can range from 10 years to up to 40 years, in the SFR space the most common fixed rate mortgage is 30 years.

PROS:

- Even if mortgage rates increase astronomically, your interest rate is locked in and your monthly payments won't change.

- Knowing how much you need to put aside for your mortgage payments every month for the next 15/30 years is incredibly helpful when it comes to budgeting for the rest of your expenses.

- The fixed rates make it easier to shop around for loans, because you can simply calculate your monthly payments and make the best choice.

CONS:

- Timing can be your worst enemy when it comes to locking in your fixed rate on a mortgage loan; you may feel you're getting a low rate at closing time, but a few months down the line the rates may drop further and you feel trapped.

- If you do choose to refinance, you may end up paying thousands to do so, and may ultimately cost you more money.

- Fixed rate mortgages generally have higher interest rates than ARMs, and if you end up selling or refinancing in the first few years, your interest payments would have been greater.

Home Inspection – After your offer to buy a home has been accepted, you'll want to have a home inspection done. This can give you a more comprehensive understanding of its condition. The home inspector's report is based on his/her visual evaluation and professional estimation of all accessible parts of the house.

Most home inspections include:

- Interior: Look at the overall condition of all interior finishes, as well as the care in everything was put together. Look for evidence of water leakage around windows, doors, and ceilings. If you detect a musty odor, this could indicate poor ventilation or the presence of mold or mildew.

- Exterior: This includes items like roofs, masonry, fascia boards, siding, rain gutters, downspouts, dangling wires, and other exterior materials. If the house looks like it needs to be painted soon, make note of that.

- Plumbing: Make note of unusual noises and odors around fixtures and pipes. Consider having the sewer line scoped for potential cracks and obstructions.
- Structure: Look for hairline cracks or more substantial damage in brick joints or poured concrete foundations. Look at the base of ceilings and walls in each room to see if there are apparent shifts in the foundation or other structural elements.

- Electrical: Check for switches that don't work or are otherwise malfunctioning. Outlets should be grounded and make sure the electrical panel is updated and expandable.

- Heating and air conditioning: Is the system doing its job sufficiently. Check the age of the equipment to determine how much life might be left.

The purpose of this inspection is so that you, the buyer, understand the cost of renovations or repairs that the house may need, in addition to the cost of the mortgage itself. The inspection report gives you a list of faults with the property that you can use to negotiate a better price with the seller.

Homeowner's Insurance – Prior to the mortgage closing date, the homeowners must secure property insurance on the new home. The policy must list the lender as loss payee in the event of a fire or other event. This must be in place prior to the loan going into

HUD (Department of Housing and Urban Development) – The Department of Housing and Urban Development (HUD) is a government agency dedicated to stimulating the housing market, strengthening communities, and fulfilling the need for affordable housing in America. The HUD is responsible for implementing national policies that address housing needs, and enforcing the programs and laws put in place. The federal agency has different programs that help the housing industry thrive on both sides, for sellers and buyers.

- Along with the FHA, it works to increase government insured housing, protecting lenders.

- It helps improve the quality of neighborhoods and recreational centers.

- The HUD helps provide mortgage insurance so more families and individuals can afford homes.

- In addition to helping with housing, the HUD has programs that provide subsidized rent for the elderly and disabled

HUD-1 Settlement Statement (Closing Sheet) – The HUD-1 Settlement Statement itemizes all final costs of processing the mortgage, and indicates whether the buyer or seller is liable to make those payments. Under the Real Estate Settlement Procedures Act (RESPA), the HUD-1 is the standard form to be used for all mortgage settlements.

You will receive this closing sheet from the closing agent. It covers all the costs that were mentioned in the Good Faith Estimate that you received 3 days after you submitted the loan application. Instead of just estimates, however, the HUD-1 has the actual costs listed alongside the previously quoted ones for easy comparison, get comfortable with this document.

As a buyer, you should look over this list with your realtor. Some of the costs can be substantially higher than what was initially quoted in the estimate, and you have the right to contest these.

Loan-to-value Ratio (LTV) – The loan-to-value ratio is a metric a lender uses to determine risk of loaning money to you as a borrower. The ratio represents the loan amount as a percentage of the property value; it is calculated by dividing the amount of money requested in the loan by the property value of the home. The property value used to calculate the ratio come from the home appraisal. Whatever number comes in the appraisal report is used by the lenders. The ratio is then sent along with the loan application for underwriting purposes after which you'll be quoted an interest rate for the loan. In addition to determining that you qualify for the loan, lenders use this ratio to calculate the costs and fees you will incur for borrowing the money.

If your LTV ratio is low, you may qualify for lower interest rates. A lower loan-to-value ratio means there is more equity on the home, and you are considered less risky to default on the loan. It also gives the lender peace of mind because if you were to default, they could sell the property in foreclosure and make up the loss. LTV ratios are also used to evaluate your mortgage insurance payments. If you make a 20 percent down payment on a conventional mortgage loan, the lenders may waive the private mortgage insurance payments. For FHA loans, borrowers are required to pay the minimum 3.5 percent down payment in order for their mortgage to be insured.

Origination Fee (Points) – The origination fee is the charge applied to a borrower to pay for the process of a mortgage application and for creating the home loan. Quoted as a percentage of the total loan amount, origination fees are usually 2 percent of the mortgage.

The origination of a mortgage loan includes everything it takes to put the mortgage in place. The process begins when you submit the loan application along with the supporting documentation. It includes your loan officer — the loan originator, who initiates and works to complete the loan— pulling up your credit score and submitting all the information to underwriter, who ultimately determines whether you qualify for the loan. The origination fee is also seen as mortgage points to be paid to the loan originator at the closing of the transaction. The fee is like other commission-based payment, and works as the loan originator's payment for selling you the loan. 'Buy down the rate by paying points. Paying a percentage point up front to get a lower rate – usually a ½ percent reduction in your interest rate will eventually be a saving to borrowers in the long run if they stay with the rental property longer than the cost to buy down the rate. Calculate what a ½ point reduction is worth vs. the 1 pt. payment to get it.

Pre-approval – A pre-approval is a statement from a potential lender asserting that a borrower would be approved for a certain loan amount. Gaining pre-approval means that you, as a borrower, likely qualify for a certain mortgage according to the lender's guidelines.

To obtain a pre-approval letter from a lender, you will be required to provide some information about your finances, and provide permission to run your credit report. After a preliminary evaluation of the information provided, the lender will state in writing that you are a pre-approved borrower. This letter will be provided to the selling agent to show capability.

It is beneficial to take the time to get pre-approved by a lender, since it will help in your search for a mortgage. The pre-approval helps you get a better idea of how much you can afford to offer on a home, and in doing so, narrow down your search. Having a pre-approval letter also indicates to sellers and mortgage lenders that your finances are credible, and you are serious about purchasing a home. The pre-approval letter is usually valid between 60 to 90 days, so it's important to request one when you know you'll have time to shop for a home. Keep in mind, however, that being pre-approved does not guarantee that you will ultimately receive the quoted interest rates, or that you may be approved for the loan. It also doesn't mean that the offer you place on a property will be accepted.

Prepayment (Loan Prepayment) – Borrowers can make prepayments on a mortgage loan by paying extra on their monthly payments toward the principal of the loan. By making larger payments, you are essentially minimizing the balance on the loan and shortening its term.

There are upsides to making prepayments on a mortgage.

- By making payments earlier than required, you are saving on the interest the mortgage is costing you; the sooner you pay off your loan, the sooner you can stop making monthly payments with interest.

- Interest that you save on a mortgage is tax-deductible. If you were investing the same money elsewhere, however, you'd be paying taxes on the income you make.

- By paying the principal loan sooner, you're increasing the equity you have on your home, and will be able to own it earlier than expected.

But then there are the downsides as well

- Some mortgages come with a prepayment penalty. The lenders charge a fee if the loan is paid in full before the term ends.

- Making larger monthly payments means you may have limited funds for other expenses. It also means that you could miss out on investing money in other ventures that could bring you a higher rate of return.

- You may have obtained an extremely low interest rate with your mortgage. In some cases, you would save more money making the regular monthly payments for a 30-year term, and using your available funds for other investments.

If you do decide to make prepayments on your mortgage, it is imperative that you point out what you want the extra money to go towards. Make sure that the extra funds go towards principal, not interest. You are not earning any equity on your home by paying interest in advance.

Principal (Loan Balance) - A loan's actual balance, excluding the interest owed for borrowing, is called the principal. This is the original amount borrowed from the lender that needs to be repaid, in addition to all the other costs of borrowing that amount (interest, insurance, and taxes). The principal is paid monthly, over the term of the mortgage.

Principal Balance is the amount left to pay on a loan. As you pay this balance, you're earning more equity on your house. However, mortgages (even fixed rate loans) are designed in a way that your initial monthly payments distribute more funds towards interest than principal.

To pay off the loan sooner, gain equity on the property, and avoid paying too much interest. Many borrowers choose to pay extra towards the principal balance every month, and this is called prepayments. It is estimated that making one additional monthly payment every year can cut down the term of the loan by five years – keep that thought in mind if you're a long-term owner.

Private Mortgage Insurance – When the loan to value (LTV) is higher than 80%, lenders will generally not be able to complete the transaction. In these cases, the borrowers can get Private Mortgage Insurance (PMI), which is a guarantee to the lender that until the borrower reaches an 80% LTV, they are covered from default. To get this protection, borrowers pay a monthly PMI premium. One popular option to get around paying PMI is to take a second mortgage and use it as a down payment on the first. Keep in mind, private money will not allow a 2nd mortgage on your property.

Property Tax – When you purchase a home, you are liable to pay property taxes on it. The governing body of the area, whether it is federal, local, state, or municipal, levies these taxes. The amount you pay in property taxes depends on the value of the house and the land on which it's built. Property tax payments gave rise to escrow accounts. Lenders include an additional amount in your monthly payments that adds up and goes into your escrow account. These funds are held in escrow until they are used to pay annual property taxes. Lenders are required to send you an end-of-year statement of your escrow account activity that gives you detailed information of how much money went towards property taxes, and other payments, such as insurance.

Lenders must worry about your property taxes on your home because it could be a liability for *them*. If you were unable to repay the loan and the lender takes back the property through foreclosure, they are liable to pay unfulfilled property tax payments on the house that were originally your responsibility. This is also one reason that not paying your property taxes could be a default, which means the lender could foreclose on your home even if you've been making principal and interest payments.

Reverse Mortgage (HECM, Home Equity Conversion Mortgage) – Like a traditional mortgage, a reverse mortgage uses your house as collateral for the loan, except in this case, your loan balance will grow because you aren't making monthly payments. The loan does not have to be paid until the borrower dies, or moves out of the property.

Reverse Mortgages are ideal for senior borrowers who have gathered a considerable amount of equity on their home. As you would imagine, life expectancy plays a big part for lenders in determining the value of the loan. Normally, the older you are and the lower loan balance you have, the more money you can expect from the lender in terms of a reverse mortgage. Many seniors opt for a reverse mortgage to borrow cash against the equity on their homes so that they can supplement their income, very popular with today's "baby boomer" generation from the 1950s and 60s.

The Home Equity Conversion Mortgage (HECM) is the only reverse mortgage insured by the FHA, and available through FHA approved lenders. If the homeowner dies or moves out permanently (this is when the borrower has not lived in the house for 12 consecutive months) the lenders are repaid through the sale of the house. Since the loan is insured, the lender is reimbursed, should the sale fall short of the loan amount. In cases where the borrower dies and has heirs, they will receive a letter from the lender about the mortgage. The heirs in this case have a few options. If the home exceeds the value of the loan balance, they can sell the property and keep the difference. Heirs can give the house to the lender if they choose not to keep it or if the balance owed is more than what it's worth. They may even choose to keep the home and pay it off themselves, in which case the amount is no more than 95 percent of the appraised value.

Second Mortgage - A second mortgage is placed on a property that is already being used as collateral for a 1st mortgage. Just like your original home loan, the second mortgage is secured by your home, and is used to repay the loan in the event of default.

Borrowers choose to take out a second mortgage on their home for different reasons. You could use it to consolidate debts of high interest into one mortgage loan with a much lower rate, or to avoid paying private mortgage insurance on your first mortgage. You also have the option to borrow cash against the equity on your home to make renovations or pay off some of your more substantial bills.

There are two types of second mortgages; a home equity loan, or a home equity line of credit (HELOC). The first type provides you a large sum of money up front. You make regular payments with a fixed interest rate to repay the loan according to the mortgage terms. The HELOC, on the other hand, usually has an adjustable interest rate, and like a credit card, lets you borrow money as you need it. Second mortgages involve the same amount of work as the first, including home appraisals, disclosures, paperwork, and a few fees. It is not necessary for the second mortgage to come from the same lender, either; you have the option to go with a different mortgage provider. So, you will have to shop for mortgages the way you did before, in order to get the best deal.

Settlement Costs - prior to closing, the attorneys involved in the mortgage closing will meet to determine the final costs that are associated with the loan. These settlement costs are given to all parties so that they will be prepared to pay the closing costs that have been agreed upon.

Title Insurance – the lender is using the home as collateral for the mortgage transaction. Because of this, they need to be certain that the title of the property is clear of any liens that could jeopardize the Mortgage. So, lenders will require borrowers to get title insurance on the property, which will ensure that the homes are free and clear.

Truth in Lending is a federal mandate that all lenders must follow. There are several important parts to the Truth in Lending regulations, including proper disclosure of rates, how to advertise mortgage loans, and many other aspects of the lending process. These regulations were put into place to protect consumers from potential fraud. It is your responsibility to read your Truth in Lending guidelines, and make sure that you are compliant.

Subprime Mortgages are loans granted to borrowers with low credit scores — usually below 600 — who would not be approved for most conventional mortgages. Because of the risk that comes with granting a loan to such borrowers, these loans generally come with high interest rates.

There are fixed and adjustable rate subprime mortgages available. The ARM is the most common type, sometimes confusing and misleading borrowers with the initial low fixed rates before proceeding jump to much higher adjustable rates, which could be a problem for the investor.

There are pros and cons to such mortgages

PROS:

- It allows people with low credit scores a chance to own a home without going through years of trying to establish a better credit history.

- Subprime loans can help borrowers fix their credit scores, by using it to pay off other debts and then working towards making timely payments on the mortgage.

CONS:

- Closing costs and fees are generally higher with subprime loans; the lender tries to get as much money up front as possible because of the increased risk and chances of the borrower defaulting.

- Even though credit scores aren't a determining factor for qualifying for the loan, income is. Borrowers must show that they have sufficient income to finance the monthly mortgage payments.

22 BONUS SECTION
STEP BY STEP PROCESS FOR PROCURING AN
ACQUISITION/REHAB –BRIDGE LOAN

I am going to walk with you through a typical deal. If you have bought several assets, or this is your first time at the rodeo, you and I will go through a simulated transaction and what you should expect. I will assume you just found a property that you want to purchase, rehab and sell, or maybe hold and rent.

Once you have located the property, you will take two steps at the same time; begin Interviewing lenders, and do the necessary property review to make an informed offer.

If you haven't found a lender leading up to the finding the property, do so as quickly as possible. Finding a local or national lender like <u>Real Estate Lender USA</u> can be done via the Internet. Your common questions should be focused on your experience, your credit score, the location of the property, the lenders maximum LTC based on the above information, and the Rate and Term. When you find a match, lock the lender in and get their required paperwork out of the way. Make sure they can provide you with a commitment letter or loan approval letter, as you will need this for the seller.

Visit the property at least three times before making an offer. The first time you'll want to go with your agent, ensuring that your agent understands your agenda. You'll need either comps of recently sold properties or average rental rates for the area if you plan on holding the asset as a rental. Take notes about the property and write down issues you can see immediately, such as missing appliances, windows, carpeting or flooring. Discuss the strength of the local market with your agent, remembering the agent is out for the commission; back up what they say with independent facts learned through your own due diligence. Also, don't be afraid to speak with local property managers if you're looking to hire one.

Your second visit within the week is with your contractor and agent. Get both involved in your vision, and have your contractor create a rough draft of a rehab budget based on your intentions. When you choose a contractor for the first time, make sure that you understand his background. Has the contractor done rehab for rental properties in the past? There is a *huge* budget difference when preparing a property for rental or for sale. I recently bought a nice property in Port Richey, Florida, and the rehab budget for the sale was $33,000 – the budget if I was going to keep it as a rental was just $22,000. Once your contractor has walked the property with you, he should go back and create the rehab budget worksheet to reflect his labor and material costs. Ensure that your contractor understands the need to be timely and accurate on the rehab budget, as you still haven't made an offer.

The third walkthrough is again with your contractor and his rehab budget. This is the occasion that you want to add or subtract rehab needs, so you can keep your project on track. Make sure the rehab budget presented to you is accurate and complete, and have the contractor sign the rehab budget.

He listed his material costs, and now you need to make sure he is not padding the price shown. Call Lowe's or Home Depot, or just go down to your local store. Grab one of the very knowledgeable sales team members and walk through the budget and compare prices. If you see a window you like and it is cheaper than the price shown on the contractor's budget, go with the lower price.

Now it's offer day. Discuss the earnest money needed at the time of the offer, and have a check ready to go with your offer and your commitment letter that shows you have the necessary funding. Your offer *must* include time for both an inspection and/or an appraisal. You need to allow yourself ample time for these events to occur, and both will take about a week from the date of ordering. Ask for a closing of least 45 days, and settle on 30 days. You need to ensure that your earnest money is refundable if the inspection or the appraisal fails to justify the price you're paying – if the seller insists that the funds are non-refundable, walk away. Sometimes the effort of saying, "no thanks" is difficult, but saying "yes" to a bad deal, knowing you're stuck in the transaction, is even worse. You need to know your minimum return on investment that you're willing to accept. Never bend below that number.

When you're making the offer, use your rehab budget and comps in the area as leverage. Don't offer the listed price – negotiate. You know what it is going to cost you to rehab, and you know the offer price you intend to list the property for when you're finished. That spread is your profit, and the lower you can move the price you pay for the property the better the spread in your favor. Don't force the process; if the price doesn't work, or you can't get where you need to be, don't compromise. Just walk away.

When your offer is accepted, the fun really begins. Get your purchase contract and rehab budget over to your lender ASAP. During the process of placing your offer, you have been gathering the necessary documents the lender will require. You can fire that information over via email the same day that your offer has been accepted, I can assure you that the lender will be very impressed with your process. I stress this next statement to my clients over and over – *don't send any documents that the lender has not requested.* I get more information than I have an interest in, such as property tax receipts, information on the home the borrower lives in, information on the broker handling the purchase for you… these are all examples of worthless information. Stick to the documents your lender has asked for, you will speed up the process and have fewer headaches.

You have already asked the lender if he is going to require a BPO or appraisal, and the lender will let you know how their schedule coincides with the ordering of this event. Be sure to have provided your credit card information so either can be ordered. During this process, you and your contractor have continued to refine your rehab budget down to the dime. He should sign the final revision and provide his contact information in case the lender needs to speak with him. The appraiser will need the rehab budget before he goes in appraise the property; if there is a tenant or owner living on the property, you will have to arrange ahead of time for this event to occur. Make sure you allow 24-48-hour notice, and everybody will be far happier.

There is a period of time that you will wait for the underwriting and appraisal process to catch up with you. This is the right time to keep doing your market research regarding sales cycles and rents in the area, watching recent sales and prices as well as taking as many photos as you can of your property before rehab starts.

You will need to choose a title company and property insurance company. Be sure you have the lender clause for title and insurance – this information can be provided by the lender to title. I always suggest you provide the contact information so lender and title can communicate.

The appraisal comes back and the price supports your request, which is a green light to close. You may have a few loose ends, but they will be minor in nature. You may be asked for a letter of explanation regarding a deposit, or an updated operating agreement on your LLC. Be sure that your good standing letter from your State is up to date – they do expire.

A typical acquisition/rehab or bridge loan should close in 21 days, and you'll need to keep your lender aware of your closing date. The close will occur at your title company, and you will be made aware of the date that has been agreed to close your transaction. Your required funds for your closing need to be wired early, so the lender knows you'll be able to comply. 2-3 days is normal.

Closing is done swiftly without a lot of drama. You will be called into the title company at the time of closing, sign and go. Congratulations – your deal is done! Ensure that you have kept your contractor up to date with the closing process, as you'll want him on the property the first available date after closing. Remember, the interest expense clock is *ticking - ticking - ticking, into the future. I had to say that, sorry.*

If you intend to keep the asset and put a tenant in place you will want to own the leased asset for *at least* five months. This will ensure that you have a seasoned asset, and your mortgage will be considered on the LTV vs. LTC – a huge benefit for you financially.

If you intend to sell the asset, get it on the market before rehab is complete. I have found that, when you involve a new owner with the final steps whereby they can make some choices, you will have a better, faster offer than waiting. I have clients that list their property when they are half finished. This way, a new buyer gets to choose the wall colors or pay for an upgrade during rehab, making it a very savvy way to do business.

Here is my last word on contractors, and the amount of time they need to complete the task. I allow 10 days per $10,000 spent on rehab. You need to have a lock down date for completion, and a penalty clause if that date passes without completion.

23 CONCLUSION

Throughout the pages of this book, I've exposed to you some of the greatest secrets, strategies, tools and techniques in order to successfully borrow the money you need from the private loan markets. You have read how rates rarely decide if your project will or won't tender a profit, and how what really matters is your ability to leverage your investment so you use less of your own money and more of the lenders capital; remember that leverage is king. Your project, if chosen properly and managed according to a solid business plan, *will* yield the returns you envision.

I've shown you things to consider, things to look out for, and how you need to up your image and demeanor on the telephone when seeking capital. Please use the tools, strategies and techniques that I have shared with you in these pages to change your life for the better. To break free of the confines of traditional banking, as the private money market and its lenders *care* about you and your projects.

You now have all the information you need, so it's time to take action and start borrowing from the private markets. Begin by putting what you've read and learned here into practice with your own investments. Private money markets are the best way that I have found during my investing career to really beat the market in a safe, secured and insured way.

I wish you the best of luck in your new approach to finding the necessary capital you need to thrive in the American Dream. I hope that you will feel free to contact me and ask me any questions that you have along the way – I am here to answer them, and to guide you and lend a helping hand to set you on your path to wealth in any way I can. Please take advantage of the opportunity to contact me, ask questions and work with me to see your dreams and goals succeed.

Anthony A. O'Brien
Real Estate Lender USA / Summit & Crowne Capital Partners
NMLS# 1473497
P.O. Box 2668 Mooresville NC 28117
855.885.9100

ABOUT THE AUTHOR

Tony O'Brien is an accomplished executive and visionary, with over 25 years of experience within the real estate/energy sector. Tony's experience covers real estate capital markets, marketing, and the purchase and sales of both SFR and multi-family investment properties for investors worldwide.

Tony brings an extensive background in capital markets, as well as acquisition/disposition assistance to the SFR and multi-family markets. His companies assist real estate investors with their funding and resell requirements, from consulting on SFR pricing, valuations and rehab to tenant occupancy. Tony has created some of the best lending products in the private money industry.

Tony's career began after college at Michigan State University with Bache, Halsey, Stuart & Shields, which would later become Prudential Bache Securities. Tony rose to the title of Senior Vice President-Institutional Sales, where he ran the capital markets operation in the Midwest.

Tony moved to San Francisco in 1985 and founded the hedge fund Spinnaker Partners, becoming a Member of the PSE, CBOE and New York Stock Exchange. Tony's primary focus was the creation of complex mathematical arbitrage, option pricing, and volatility models for both hedge and trading opportunities within equity markets. Tony's focus included risk management and price arbitrage between various equity relationships as well as their derivatives through open outcry markets on the CBOE, PSE, AMEX, and the NYSE.

Tony is the founder and Managing Partner of Real Estate Lender USA wholly owned by Summit & Crowne Capital Partners LLC. The leader in one stop lending from acquisition rehab – bridge – Transactional – Term Mortgages. Tony authors a successful real estate newsletter related to investment properties, property analysis, capital markets, and lending criteria

Anthony A. O'Brien

Made in the USA
San Bernardino, CA
30 April 2020